Midnight Magic

by

Sara Bourgeois

D1527316

Chapter One

"I haven't grown at all!" Meri bemoaned.

"No, I think you've grown a little," I said.

"Kinsley, I've been measuring every single day. I haven't grown one millimeter."

It had been six months since I'd done the spell that turned Meri into a kitten, and everyone thought that he'd just grow up again. We hadn't been able to find a spell or ritual that could reverse the one I did to make him a kitten in the first place, but we did assume it would work itself out.

That hadn't happened.

It seemed that I had permanently turned him into a kitten. He'd accepted the change when he thought it was temporary, but upon the realization that he might never grow…

Meri was losing it.

I really wished I had time that morning to indulge his neurosis, but I had to go. My new shop, Summoned Goods & Sundries had taken off, I'd been busier than I ever expected.

There was also a new shop opening across the square from mine, and I wanted to be there to celebrate with the new owner. Nobody had any idea what the shop would be. The space next to the Brew Station had opened up when a little sewing shop closed, and a new tenant had rented it. Viv, the owner of the Brew Station, and I were dying to know what was going in there. The sign was being hung that morning just in time for the grand opening.

I planned on taking over a gift basket of candles and oils, and Viv was taking coffee and pastries. We planned on welcoming the new business with open arms. I had gotten to know Astra Argent after she'd moved into town. She was a regular at both the Brew Station and my store.

"We have to go to work," I said. "Are you coming with me?"

"I suppose," Meri said. "Do you think Viv will have bacon for me?"

"Meri, you just had breakfast."

"What? I'm a growing boy."

I wanted to argue that point so badly, but I kept it to myself. I wanted Meri to go with me that day, and if I ticked him off, he'd probably stay home. Or, we'd just argue more and leave Viv standing there waiting for us.

"I'm sure she will," I said. "She always does, right?"

"Yeah, that's the only good thing about my new stature. I do get a lot of treats."

With that, we headed out for the day. When we arrived in the square, I parked my car in front of my shop. The canvas covering the new store's name was still in place, so we hadn't missed the big unveiling.

I was so excited not only to have a new witch in town, but also a new business in the square. I hoped that Viv, Astra, and I could all form an alliance to help each other out. Viv had helped me out a great deal in the beginning, and I sent as many customers her way as I could. I was fully prepared to do the same for Astra. Speculation was that she was opening a candy shop or perhaps some other type of quick service food to cater to tourists looking for snacks.

We'd had an awesome candy store when I was a young girl, but Ruby had left Coventry to take care of her mother years back. She'd opened her shop in Florida, where her mom lived, and it had thrived. There was little chance she'd ever return to Coventry.

As I walked quickly across the square, Viv emerged from the Brew Station. For a brief moment, as I walked over it, I felt the power of the ley line under Coventry surge through me. The longer I was in town and the more I embraced my craft, the more intense the feeling of being near it grew to be.

"Good morning!" I called out to Viv as I crossed the street and joined her on the sidewalk outside of the new shop. "How are you today?"

"It's a beautiful morning," she said and handed me a coffee and a white paper bag. "And yes, there's bacon in there for the little one."

I was amazed at how easily people just accepted that the cat I was with was now a kitten. The magical veil over the town was an incredible thing. No one even asked.

"Thank you so much," I said. "You'll have to let me pay you when we're done here. I don't want to be a freeloader."

"Nonsense," Viv said with a shake of her head. "But you can let me come over to your shop and grab another bag of that sea salt and lavender bath soak. That stuff is amazing."

"Of course," I said.

A crowd was beginning to form around the store as it got closer to the grand opening and the final reveal. The event had been included in the local paper and on several of the neighborhood websites. Coventry was one of the last towns in the entire country to still have a physical paper, and the ironic thing was that it had begun within the last few years.

The Coventry Conjurer was created specifically for nostalgia and to play off the town's witchy reputation. It was also a bit of a gossip rag, but that went over well in a small town like ours. Sometimes it did report on actual events like Astra's store opening.

Locals standing around watching drew in the tourists as well, and pretty soon there was a huge gathering that filled the sidewalk and spilled over into the square. People were waiting on both sides of the street for Astra to pull down the canvas and show us her new store.

Additionally, there were giant pieces of cardboard covering the store's windows from the inside. Those would be taken down once the store's name was revealed, and everyone would finally see what was inside. Would it be worth all the hype?

At first, I'd thought all of the secrecy was kind of silly, but seeing the crowd that the little mystery had drawn told me that it was a shrewd marketing move after all.

Astra emerged from the shop, and Viv and I approached her. "We come bearing gifts for our new business neighbor," Viv said.

"Yes, we wanted to officially welcome you to our business community," I added.

Viv handed Astra the food she'd brought and I handed her my gift basket. It was a fancier version of the swag bags I'd be handing out at the Midnight Magic Festival.

"Oh, thank you both so much," Astra said. "You two are so kind. I'm so glad you gave these to me before the big reveal."

"Of course," I said not quite understanding what she meant, but at the time, it didn't sound sinister. "You've been over in my shop so much. I included some of the things that seemed like your favorites."

"That's quite a gesture," she said to me and then turned to Viv. "And thank you so much for hyping my business up for me. I have a feeling this is all going to pay off for me soon."

Viv and I shot each other a look, but I just shrugged. Astra was a bit quirky, that was for sure. We were certain she'd find her place in Coventry, though. The town was full of quirky people.

Before Viv and I could say anything else to each other or to Astra, she turned to face the crowd. "Is everybody ready?" Astra called out.

A bunch of people said "Yeah!" in response.

No one was quite sure what they were excited about, but they were still enthusiastic. The anticipation was buzzing through the crowd like a hive of bees.

"I just want to let everyone know that for the first hour of the grand opening, everything in the store is 50 percent off. As long as you're in line by the time the hour is up, you get the discount. So, all you great folks are getting a great deal just for being here to support me."

People actually cheered. They were cheering for getting 50 percent off, but nobody knew on what. It seemed silly, but then again, I felt myself getting keyed up too. After all, even I loved a good sale.

"Just do it already," Viv whispered into my ear. "I'm going to have a line out the door if I don't get back soon. Charles will be flailing around dramatically at the notion he has to work."

Charles was her only day-shift employee that worked during opening hours with her. It would be another half an hour before her second employee came in to help with the morning rush.

I chuckled, but it was short-lived. Astra finally pulled a rope that was hanging from the canvas covering her sign. The whole thing fell away and revealed the name of her store. At the same time, my stomach dropped. My intuition knew something was wrong before my conscious mind could piece what I was seeing together.

The Summoning Scroll

At first, I thought that perhaps it was just a metaphysical bookstore. I sold books in my store but having a competing book shop wouldn't be so bad.

But then Astra walked into her store and took down the cardboard covering the big front windows. Her shop was just like mine. I could see the shelves filled with crystals, herbs, potion bottles, and books. Most of the items near the front were the same as my most popular goods.

She hadn't been spending time in my store because she liked it, she'd been spying on my business. The stuff in her gift basket, that I'd thought she loved, was displayed in her front window. She'd figured out my most popular sellers and put them on full display.

I could do the same thing, but it occurred to me that I'd look like I was copying her. She'd put me in the position to look like the bad guy, but as my temper rose, I felt my concern over my reputation begin to erode. The spark of annoyance in my gut was about to turn into a raging fire.

It took a moment for what was happening to register with Viv, but when it did, she let out a gasp. I felt myself grow furious and nauseated at the same time. Viv's arm shot out to support me when I wobbled a little. I wasn't faint, but the wrath in me had turned into an actual fever. I was burning with anger, and I had to get a lid on it before I began to shoot actual flames.

Astra came back outside with a huge Cheshire cat grin on her face. People in the crowd were a bit stunned at first, but the lure of 50 percent off was more than most could resist. The tourists had no idea what was going on and happily filed into the store. Some of the locals went in too, though they wouldn't look at me.

Astra approached us. "I hope you don't mind," she said to me, "but this gift basket will be perfect for a giveaway in my store. I'll do a raffle."

My hands itched and tingled, and somewhere in the dark parts of my brain, I knew the only thing that would make it stop was for me to wrap them around her devious little throat. I balled my hands into fists and fought the urge to strangle Astra, but that only made me want to punch her.

A second later, I felt Viv's hand around my arm. She was dragging me away toward the Brew Station.

"Let me go," I growled.

"No, honey. No," Viv said as soothingly as she said. "Not right now. We're going to go have some tea, and if you still want to kill her, then I'll help you."

11

"I am absolutely not going to go have tea while she does this to me," I said and yanked my arm away from Viv. Probably a little too hard, and the guilt from that turned down the gas feeding my rage.

"Please," Genevieve pleaded.

"I won't kill her. I promise. But I am going to say something. I will not just let her do this and skulk off like a wounded dog."

I took a deep breath, and I could almost see the flames behind my eyes reflected in Viv's pupils. That was all in my mind's eye, though. It had to be.

"All right. I guess we're doing this then," Viv said and straightened her back. "You have to keep it together, Kinsley. You cannot sink to her level."

I held my head up high, and we marched into The Summoning Scroll.

The place was pretty packed because most of the people outside had funneled into the shop. A few people, who I assumed were loyal to me, had just shaken their heads in disdain and walked away.

Astra wasn't going to get any business from the witches of Coventry. None of them would dare cross me or my family, but she could steal tourism business. People who just liked herbs, crystals, and candles might go to her as well. Many of the humans of Coventry were deferential to the Skeenbauers, but not all.

That wasn't the point, though. I made money at my shop, but I didn't need to earn a living there. The point was Astra was a snake that pretended to be my friend and then stabbed me in the back. She was either deliberately trying to hurt me, or she didn't care who she hurt. Either way, that was not the sort of malarkey we needed in Coventry.

She was still smiling that infuriating Cheshire cat smile as she rang up customers. The look on her face told me she was excited to see me instead of concerned. I had to take another deep breath. If I raged against her the way I wanted to, she would use that to further damage my business and advance her own.

My shop was one of the first truly successful things I'd done in my life, and I could not allow Astra to push me into burning it down.

"Stay calm," Viv said as if she'd picked up on my thoughts.

I barely heard her over the din of customers shopping and chatting, but I did hear her. I took another breath, and I felt myself relax a little more when Meri's paw darted out of my purse and touched my hand.

"Astra, this isn't funny," I said as I shouldered my way up to the empty part of the counter.

"No one is trying to be funny," she said. "But I do need you to step to the back of the line. I'll get to everyone. There's no reason to butt in."

"I'm not butting in," I said. "And, I'm certainly not here to buy anything from you."

"You need to get control of yourself, Kinsley. We're all here to have a good time and get some great deals, and you're ruining the mood."

People around us started murmuring, and I could tell the crowd was quickly going to turn against me. My only choice was to state my claim quickly and calmly.

"You knew that opening this business right across the street from mine would probably hurt my shop," I said. "And you pretended to be my friend to get information."

"Don't be such a child," Astra sniped. "This little temper tantrum you are throwing isn't a very becoming look on you."

And that was it. Something snapped in my brain. My face grew hot again, and I felt like I could spit fire. Instead of flames, it was venom. "You're going to regret doing this to me," I yelled. "You have no idea who you are dealing with, but you're going to find out. You messed with the wrong... woman. I won't let you do this. Watch your back, Astra Argent."

I turned and stormed out of the shop before Astra could say anything else. Admittedly, the last part was a little over the line. Okay, all of it had been over the line. The part about her having no idea who she was dealing with had to be true, though.

It was strange that a witch had decided to mess with me and my family, so that was the only explanation I could think of as to why she would risk ticking me off. How she didn't know who the Skeenbauers were was a mystery. Maybe she did know and wasn't smart enough to care.

The part about me not letting her get away with it was true too if for no other reason than I wouldn't allow such unsavory behavior to stand in Coventry. I wasn't the sheriff or anything like that, but as the head of the coven, I was a de facto leader of sorts. It wasn't as if I'd taken up that mantle yet, but I thought perhaps Astra's shenanigans would be the thing that made me finally step up.

"You should come get that tea now," Viv said as soon as we were outside.

"I suppose it wouldn't hurt if I delay opening my store for a little while," I said.

"I think it's best. I don't want you going over there and stewing all day. I can just see you at your window staring across the square," she said.

I wanted to protest, but she was right. That's most likely exactly what I would have done. I chuckled at the mental image of me standing in my store window glaring at Astra's shop all day. "All right. One cup of tea, and then I do have to go to work. I'm sure there are some people who will still shop at my store. I'd better not let them down. I'll need every customer I can get until I fix this."

"You're going to run her out of town, aren't you?" Viv asked as I followed her into the Brew Station.

"That's the plan," I responded. "Do you think less of me?"

"Not for one second, Kinsley. I'm just glad I've got a front row seat to the fireworks," Viv said. "Now, let me get you a hazelnut latte."

"I thought you said I should have tea."

"Do you want tea?" she asked and then cut me off before I could answer. "Somehow I doubt it. Let me get you what you really want."

"I knew there was a reason I loved you," I said. "Thank you so much."

Chapter Two

I'd been right about people still coming to my shop. There were even a couple of witches waiting outside for me to open when I left the Brew Station.

"Here she comes," I heard one of them whisper as I crossed the street.

It wasn't in a mocking tone, but instead, they seemed like they were waiting for the storm. I wasn't entirely sure if they were actually there to buy anything, or if they just wanted a front row seat to my volcanic eruption.

After all, the head of the Skeenbauer Coven, whatever that meant, and the most powerful witch anyone had ever heard of, whatever that meant, had to put on a pretty good show when she blew her top. Fireworks, as Viv had described.

Unfortunately for them, Meri's soothing magic was better than expected, and by the time I reached the front door of my shop, I felt much better. I'd hoped they had some purchases in mind, or they were going to be bitterly disappointed. I would not lose it in my shop in front of my customers. If anything, life had made me stronger than that.

"Good morning, folks," I said as I put the key in the lock and opened the door. "I won't forget your loyalty, and to reward you, I'm also having a 50 percent off sale for the next hour. I'm not going to make a big announcement in the square or anything, but if you want to call your friends or family and let them know, please do."

And some of them did call friends and family. The shop filled up after a few minutes. It wasn't nearly the amount Astra had across the street, but it was enough to make me feel even better.

Eventually, Astra's sale ended and the crowd in her shop thinned out considerably. By lunchtime, I'd stopped watching. I was going to head over to the Brew Station for a sandwich, but Reggie showed up with bags from the diner.

"I brought burgers and waffle fries," she said and set the white paper bags on the counter.

"Thank you," I said. "You didn't have to do that."

"Eh, it's not like I paid for them. I put my last order of the day in wrong and these are the castoffs," she said.

"You know, I think that's technically stealing," I said.

"I didn't do it on purpose," Reggie said and rolled her eyes.

"Sure."

"You totally did it on purpose," Meri said as he jumped up on the counter. "You're such a bad liar."

"Your voice sounded weird there," Reggie said because she had no idea it was Meri that had insulted her.

"I think I'm getting a bit of a cold." Then I was the bad liar, but to sell the story, I let out a fake cough followed by a sniffle.

"I'm sure you have something around this shop that can take care of that," she said. "Don't you have some healing herbs or that tea you're always trying to get me to drink? That ecanation or something."

"Speaking of which, are you going to hang around after we eat and help me put together more swag bags?" I asked. "Or do you have pressing afternoon engagements?"

"That's why I'm here," she said. "Are you putting the ecanation tea in the bags?"

"It's echinacea, and yes, I'm including a tea sampler."

"Right, echinacea and chamomile," Reggie said.

"I'm also putting in the citrus splash and a couple of sachets of kava tea."

"Ohh, kava's the good stuff, right?"

"It helps with anxiety," I said. "It also numbs the stomach, so it's good for tummy troubles."

"We should have a cup," Reggie hinted.

"How about after we work on the bags? I don't want you zoning out on me. The festival is coming up faster than I'm prepared for," I said.

The Midnight Magic Festival was a Coventry tradition that went back around seven years, but the town liked to let the tourists think it had been happening for centuries. Since I was one of the newest businesses in Coventry, I'd been offered the honor of providing gift bags to festival attendees. At my expense, of course. I didn't mind, though. It was good advertising, and Meri had helped me dig up some money to pay for the items and the bags. Hangman's House had a way of providing.

Thorn had encouraged me to petition the town council to pay for the swag bags since it benefited the town for me to hand them out, but the problem was that the council had disbanded years ago. At least, they hadn't met for a long time, and everything seemed to be run, on the surface, by the elected mayor.

Of course, things were actually run by Amelda and my mother, but that was a whole different story. The layers of political intrigue in Coventry were as thick and fluffy as marshmallows, but I wasn't interested in any of it. I needed to take an interest in it, but my mother and great-grandmother did an excellent job until I was ready.

Either way, I didn't need the money, and I wasn't going to wade into those waters. Petitioning the council for money would resurrect them, and the word around town was that there had been some sort of major clash between them and Amelda a few years after I left town. She won, and they stopped meeting. Coventry didn't need that kind of drama rising from the grave.

What I needed was to finish the bags before the festival. It was boring, tedious work that probably would have gone a lot faster if I'd just used magic, but I had a policy of not using magic unless it was necessary.

I thought that other witches were way too loose with it, and I wanted to be more disciplined. Or perhaps it was just because I'd lived my adult life until I moved back to Coventry without magic, and I wasn't quite comfortable yet with who I really was.

That and Reggie really wanted to help with the bags. She picked up on what was going on in Coventry more than most people, but she still didn't come out and admit that magic and the paranormal were real. I hadn't decided when or if I was ever going to tell her. The same for Viv. I'd become close friends with both women over the last few months, but I had to hide a big part of myself from them. Life would have been easier if I'd just made friends with witches, but that wasn't what the universe had in store for me.

"Earth to Kinsley," Reggie said with a chuckle. "I think you spaced out."

"Oh, sorry," I said. "Well, since there's no one in the shop, why don't we go in the back and get started with the bags. We can leave the door open in case someone comes in."

"Can't we just do it out here?" Reggie said. "You've got all this counter space."

She waved her hand over the expanse of counter. I noted the apprehension in her eyes as well. No one liked being in the back of the store. I didn't mind so much because I knew the ghost was more of a nuisance than anything else, but its presence freaked out all of the normal folks.

"Sure, let me bring the boxes of stuff and the bags up here," I said.

"I can help with that," Reggie said nervously. "We just have to grab stuff and bring it out, right?"

"Yeah," I said. "Are you okay?"

"I'm fine. It's just that back room freaks me out. I don't know what it is. I always feel like something's watching me or about to pop out around the corner."

"I hear you. That's why I get to rent this place so cheap. You're not the only one who feels that way," I responded. "Yeah, there are two boxes and the big bag of gift bags. They're right by the door. We don't even have to go all the way in."

"Have you ever seen anything back there?" Reggie asked as we made our way through the shop. "I mean, you feel it when you're back there too, right? I don't know how you work in that office."

I turned back to look at her just in time to watch her shiver. For the first time in a long time, I felt the hair on the back of my neck stand up. The ghost that haunted my shop was winding up to do something.

Fortunately, I'd placed the boxes of stuff for the bags and the bag of gift bags near the door. I lifted the first box and handed it to Reggie quickly. Then I grabbed the other box and the bags and shut the door behind us. I didn't even have to tell Reggie to move. As soon as she had her box in hand, she was on her way back to the front of the shop.

At some point, I needed to do something about the ghost. I either had to send them packing with magic, or I had to find out what they wanted. Ironically, Astra had bought me some time. I'd been thinking about hiring someone for a while, but if she put a dent in my business, it meant I didn't need an assistant quite as fast. It all depended on how successful her shop was. Given that it was right next door to the Brew Station, I imagined it would be popular.

But if I couldn't get rid of the ghost, I'd just have to find a witch who wanted to work in my shop with me. That wouldn't have been that hard. I could hire a teenager or a retiree. Heck, Lilith probably would have done it if I let her have wine in the shop.

It was an issue that would wait a few days until after the festival. Reggie and I spent the afternoon putting the bags together, and then I went home. I'd invited her over, but she said she had somewhere to be.

I had a feeling it had something to do with a guy, but she wasn't being forthcoming about it. I'd considered pressing the issue, but she'd tell me when she was ready.

Thorn and I hadn't gone out for a few days, so I halfway expected him to show up or at least call. We'd gotten to a point where we never went a day without talking, but he ended up having to work late a lot. He needed to hire a new deputy for the evening shift, and until he did, those hours were his.

After dinner, I still hadn't heard from Thorn, but there was a knock at my front door. I checked my phone as I got off the sofa, and there wasn't a text from him either.

I supposed Thorn just dropping by wasn't that unusual. He normally called or texted first, but I reasoned that he'd forgotten.

As I made my way over to the door, Meri shot out from one of his wall tunnels and put himself between me and my destination.

"What are you doing?" I asked.

"Don't answer that," he said.

"It's probably just Thorn. What's wrong with you?"

"It's not Thorn," Meri said. "It's something else. It's… It's a vampire."

I'd been reaching for the door, but I pulled my hand back. I hadn't heard from or seen Azriel for months. As quickly as he'd come into my life, he'd disappeared. It was almost as if I'd never met him, and to be honest, I'd nearly forgotten him. At least, I'd managed to push him to the back of my mind. He wasn't the kind of man you could totally forget.

"Do you think it's Azriel?" I asked. "I don't know what other vampire would come to my house."

"Just check before you open the door," Meri said. "And if it is him, call Thorn."

"Why would I call Thorn?"

"He said he'd be the one who would fulfil your obligation to Azriel. I think you should let him do it," Meri said.

"You think that's why he's here?" I asked. "Wait, I don't even know if it's him. We're getting ahead of ourselves."

As I said the last part, whoever was on the other side of the door pounded insistently. It made me jump about a foot off the ground.

"Kinsley, I can hear you in there. Please open the door." It was Azriel, and he sounded scared.

I stepped over Meri and opened the door without thinking. Something in his voice drove me to act. Something in Azriel's tone made it okay for me to be stupid, and I had no idea how dangerous that could really be.

He was even paler than I remembered, and his black irises were nearly gray. Azriel looked sick, and that was so unexpected that it took my breath away.

"Azriel, what is it? Please, come in," I said.

"No, I can't. You have to come with me. Please," he begged and reached for my hand.

"Come with you? Where?" I shook my head no, but even as I resisted, I took a step toward him.

I stopped short of taking his hand, though. My palm itched with the anticipation of touching his, and I had to fight not to give in. Every fiber of me suddenly longed for him, but I knew better. It was how a predator drew in prey.

"To the clubhouse. Please, come with me. I need you now." The desperation in his voice was thick.

"I want to help you, but you have to tell me what's going on. You're scaring me. I haven't seen you for months, and now you show up on my porch demanding I come with you."

"I'm calling in my favor," he said. "I have to. It's not for me. It's for my dog. Please, Kinsley. You have to help her."

"Your dog?" I asked, but I took another step to him. He seemed so vulnerable, and it was unexpected.

"Tangerine. I call her Geri. She got out of the club because one of those idiots left the door open too long. I never should have taken her over to the club. She got hit by a car. I tried to save her, but I can't. Please, you have to help her."

"Yes," I said and scooped up Meri. "I can help you."

Azriel was far less frightening when he was begging me to save his dog. A dog named Tangerine, no less. I followed him out to his black Mercedes and slipped into the passenger side as he held the door for me. "You in?" he asked and then closed the door gently when I nodded yes.

He drove us to the old factory so fast that I wanted to warn him not to get pulled over, but I didn't. We didn't see Thorn's cruiser at all, and I couldn't think about what would happen if Thorn pulled us over and found me in the car. It would have been difficult to explain. While I could tell him the truth, I wasn't sure that would pacify his disappointment in finding me with Azriel again.

I was glad he didn't catch us. Not because he would have been angry, he would have been, but because it would have cost us time. By the way Azriel was acting, time was something we didn't have.

He'd called in his favor, and I would do everything within my power to save Tangerine. Actually, I would have done that anyway. Not just for him, but for the dog too. *It's not like you'd do anything for him*. I told myself. I knew it was just his allure working on me.

When Azriel pulled into the lot, he kept going past the area where all of the bikes were lined up out front. We went around back, and I got out of the car before he had a chance to open the door for me.

The back lot of the old factory wasn't paved, and tiny pieces of white gravel crunched beneath my feet as I followed Azriel up a set of concrete stairs and across what had once been a loading dock.

A red exit sign glowed over the metal door we went through. Inside, I could hear the music coming from the club, but it was faint. If you didn't know any better, you'd have thought it was a radio, set on low volume, left on in another room.

The lights were quite dim until Azriel hit a switch. I found myself standing in what was just a normal kitchen. Through a doorway ahead of me was a living room. The floors were covered in dark hardwood that shone in the soft overhead lights. The furniture was black and modern. It reminded me of something you'd see in one of those snooty architectural magazines. Not what I would have expected in what I presumed was Azriel's home.

I heard a whimpering sound coming from deeper inside the building, but I wasn't sure from where. "Where is she?" Her pained cry made me feel suddenly anxious.

"This way," Azriel said.

He led me out of the kitchen, through the living room, and down a hallway to a bathroom on the right. The sound of the whimpering got louder as we approached. I barely noticed the red brocade wallpaper and huge painting of dark forests that hung on the walls as we passed.

Inside the bathroom was a tiny orange Pomeranian lying on a towel. She tried to look up when we came into the room and just collapsed back down with another whimper.

I rushed to her side and knelt. My knees hit the white tile floor a little too hard, but I ignored the sting.

Meri joined me but he sat opposite me near her head. I was surprised when he put a paw on her shoulder and started to lick her fur near her ear. He had already begun to heal her and provided little Geri with comforting pain relief magic. Her breathing immediately slowed from a shallow, panicked pant to deeper, slower breaths.

With my hands covering what looked like the worst of her wounds, I focused on the white light inside of me and channeled it into Tangerine. Something inside of her resisted me, and I began to feel nauseated. Still, I pushed through and let the healing light flow from in me into her as best I could.

Her wounds closed and the last of her whimpers stopped, but Tangerine's breathing grew erratic again. It sounded like she was drawing her last breaths, but that couldn't be.

"What's going on?" Azriel asked.

His voice was even more terrified than before, and that's when I noticed the little dog's eyes. The light was leaving them like a dying candle. She flickered out the next instant. Tangerine was still with us one second and then gone the next.

"I don't understand," I said as I stood up and backed away from her. "I healed her. How could she have died?"

Azriel took a shuddering breath. "I tried to turn her. I was panicked, and I just didn't want her to die. But we can't change animals," he said and I looked over to see reddish tears streaking down his face.

"That must have been it," I said. "I healed her, but because of the vampire blood, I couldn't keep her alive. The two magics must have opposed each other. I'm sorry."

It was my turn to take a shuddering breath. The sadness was almost overwhelming, and I realized I was feeling some of Azriel's grief as well. The pain in my chest was nearly unbearable. If he weren't a vampire, I would have been worried he was literally dying. I barely knew him, but how much he loved that little dog still came as a shock to me. It was a most unexpected discovery given that I was dealing with the undead leader of a criminal biker gang.

I reached out to him and took his hand. The gesture caught me off guard, but I couldn't let go. I didn't know why I was so easily able to feel his emotions, but I could, and it felt like he was in danger of drifting away. Or losing his mind. Either way, I was his tether in that moment. We stood there that way for a few minutes, and then Azriel changed.

Not physically, for the most part. He didn't morph into a monster or anything, but I felt his sorrow burn away. His hand had been so cold when I took it, but now it was scorching hot.

I looked over at him, and his eyes were black. Not like normal where just the pupils and irises were black. The whites had turned as dark as night as well.

"Azriel?"

"You have to do something," he snarled. "She was the only one who loved me. I didn't protect her, but I will not fail her."

"I can't do anything," I said. "I'm sorry, but she's gone."

"Don't play stupid with me, Kinsley. You have magic that can fix this. That's why I came to you and not one of the other witches in this town. Bring her back."

"What?" I asked. "You mean, necromancy? You want me to bring her back from the dead?"

"You can and you will," he said in a calm voice that simmered with barely contained wrath. "Do it now."

"Azriel, I know you're hurting, but I can't do that. I'm not a necromancer. It's not good for me to dabble in dark things."

"I'm calling in my favor, Kinsley. I don't care what you have to do, but you're going to save her. If it is in your power, then you will do it. If it is not, then you had better find someone who can," he hissed.

The thing was, I could do it. I didn't know a lot of necromancy, but Lilith had gifted me chaos and reign over the shadow things when I was young. I could bring Tangerine back, but I shied away from even using light magic for anything but what was absolutely necessary. Was I really going to use dark magic to bring Azriel's dog back from the other side?

Azriel's eyes were still blacked out and his nostrils flared with every breath, but the fury in him began to retreat. The longer he looked at me, the harder it was for him to hold onto his anger. In its place, the pain came crashing back like a tsunami. It was almost as if I could feel his soul ripping away in places. Love, even for a dog, was the only thing keeping him from turning into a monster.

Not only could I not let that happen, I didn't think I could just walk away from Tangerine either. I'd seen the pain and fear in her little eyes. She wanted to live. I'd felt her fighting for her life, and it affected me deeply.

"Do you have any black candles?" I asked.

"Are you joking?" Azriel asked as he finally let go of my hand. "I hate to be a cliché, but I am a vampire, Kinsley. All I have are black candles."

"Right. Dumb question. Okay, please get me as many black candles as you can and carry Tangerine out into the living room. I need more room than this. We have to work quickly. The tether is fading every moment."

He nodded to me and scooped up Tangerine's little body. I followed as he took her into the living room and kicked his coffee table out of the way. He laid her down and then started to leave to get the candles.

"While you're getting the candles, I'm going to go through your kitchen and see what I can find. Is that okay?"

"Whatever you have to do," he said.

In the kitchen I found a bottle of red wine, a few herbs, salt, and black pepper. It wasn't ideal, but it would work. I took what I'd gathered into the living room and arranged the herbs, salt, and peppercorns into a large circle around the dog.

When I'd finished with the circle, I poured the wine into the glass and took a huge gulp of it. After a deep breath, I drained the glass and poured another.

"Are you getting drunk?" Azriel asked as he returned with a box of candles.

"Just a little," I said. "It helps me cross the veil. I'd normally use some jimsonweed or maybe psychedelic mushrooms, but I'm working with what I have."

"How does hallucinating help you?" he asked as he set the box of candles on the floor next to me.

"Those things don't make you hallucinate," I said. "People think they do, but what they are actually doing is opening you up to the other side. People don't realize how powerful or dangerous it is. They think it's imagination, but it's not. The things that you see are real."

"I could probably come up with some mushrooms or LSD," Azriel said. "I'd just need to go ask around. Would LSD work too?"

"The wine will do," I said. "Let me set up these candles. We need to get started."

"What can I do?" Azriel asked.

"Does the wine have any effect on you?" I asked.

"Some but not as much as it would on you."

"Okay, well, finish the bottle then, and you can help me set up the candles."

He drank the wine, and we arranged the candles into the shape of a pentagram.

"Do you need anything else?" Azriel asked when the pentagram was done.

"This should do it," I said to him and then turned to Meri. "Are you up for this?"

"What's a little necromancy amongst friends?" he asked. "I'll do my best to keep anything nasty from coming through when the veil is down, but you'll need to act fast. The longer it's open, the more that will come."

"What will come?" Azriel asked.

"Demons, evil spirits," I said. "Heck, just regular spirits who are curious or want to be on this side. We have to keep all of that from crossing over and just bring Tangerine back."

"You can do that?" He sounded unsure for the first time.

"You wouldn't have come to me if I couldn't," I said. "Is the wine having any effect on you?"

"A little. What does it matter?"

"Because you'll be the one calling her back. I'll open the veil with magic, and you have to call her back to you. So, I need you to be able to see the other side. Shouldn't be hard as you live half in and half out. I need matches or a lighter," I said but then thought better of it. "You know what? Never mind." I snapped my fingers and all the candles lit at once.

"Kinsley," Azriel said breathlessly.

It was obvious he was awestruck by what I'd just done. I would have thought it would take more to impress someone who had lived for so long, but he probably hadn't spent much time around witches. Historically, we didn't mix well with vampires, but I didn't know why. Perhaps it was related to how we reacted to each other. I wasn't prepared to accept that it was just Azriel that I experienced a stark connection with, but it wasn't the time for those thoughts. There was an important task at hand.

"Focus," I said. "You can be astounded by my powers or whatever once we have Tangerine back."

"What do I do?" he asked. "How do I help?"

"You stay inside the circle and wait quietly until I say. When I give the word, you call her back. She'll come to you, but she has no idea who I am. Otherwise, I'd tell you to wait outside."

"I'm sorry I didn't ask this before, but are you in any danger? Can you be hurt by this?" Azriel asked.

"I should be fine. I have Meri to protect me, and there's not much out there that can overpower me."

"But it's not for certain?" Azriel asked.

"Nothing is."

He looked back and forth between me and Tangerine as if for the first time he realized he could be trading me for the dog's life. Azriel's face was tormented with conflict. He hadn't thought this thing through, but instead had acted on pure emotion. I wasn't angry at him for that. I couldn't be. It happened to us all.

"I don't know if I can let you do this…" He sounded as if all the fight had gone out of him.

"We've come this far, and we're going to see it through. I'll bring her back to you," I said. "I can handle this."

I could already feel the chaos seeping into me, the prick of darkness boosting my hubris. I had to keep control and not let it get its hooks into me entirely. The darkness promised power, but if you let it, it would consume you.

"Okay," he said. "Let's do it."

I focused all of my attention on thinning the veil and murmured words of chaos that I'd only ever heard Lilith use. I'd seen her reach out to the shadows a few times as a child, and I knew which words were the key. Words that cannot be written down but must only be whispered in the quiet of the night.

I could feel the veil thin to the point of being threadbare. The pull of the other side was as intense for me as it must have been for the dead to our side. I resisted the call of its mystery. I wasn't going to find out what happened if I answered the call and crossed over. I had too much to live for, but I did have to remind myself more than once. The allure of the hereafter was seductive to someone with chaos in their blood. It didn't help that I'd crossed the line and actually used necromancy. Azriel had been right to be worried. I needed to finish the ritual and disconnect myself from the darkness.

"Call her now," I said as I felt the opening begin to contract. I'd opened it as far as I could. All we could do was hope it was enough.

"Tangerine," Azriel said and then whistled. "Come here, girl."

I heard a happy bark and felt my heart lift a little. She was still close, and she'd heard him. I also felt the nasty, oily muck of something evil creeping closer.

"Call her again. We need her to come through now. I have to close the passage," I said.

"Tangerine. Come here, pretty girl," he called out. "Do you want some cheese?"

With that, I heard more happy barking and the sound of tiny claws clicking towards us. A moment later, the transparent specter of Tangerine emerged as if from thin air.

She walked over and pantomimed sniffing her body, and a second later she was pulled back into it. The tether was thankfully still intact, and it brought body and spirit back as one without the little dog having to understand what was going on.

As soon as she stood up and ran to Azriel, I let the veil close. Not a second too soon as I felt the icy fingers of something just beyond what I could see reach out for me.

I snapped my fingers again and the candles went out. By that time, Tangerine was in Azriel's arms licking his face happily.

When I recognized it was over, I collapsed onto the floor. I didn't pass out or anything, but I was just sitting there cross-legged and staring into space. I'd never felt so drained in my life. I put my hands on my knees to keep from folding over and sprawling on the floor.

Meri ran over and rubbed against my leg. It made me feel a little better, but I was still bone-tired. My eyes and body were in a competition as to which felt heavier.

"Are you all right?" Azriel asked.

He sat down on the floor next to me with Tangerine in his lap. I reached over and scratched her behind the ear, and in return, she let out a happy yip.

"That took a lot out of me," I said. "I need something to eat and I need to rest. Can you take me home?"

My eyes started to drift shut, and I almost fell over backward. Fortunately, the feeling of falling snapped me back to attention, but it would only last so long.

Azriel stood up and offered me his hand. "Why don't you rest on the sofa for a bit. I'll send one of my men out for food. You can eat and then I'll take you home."

"I have food at home. I'll be all right until we get there."

"I'm not leaving you alone like this," Azriel said and used the hand that wasn't holding Tangerine to pull me to my feet. "You can eat here, and when I'm sure you're fine, I'll take you home. You saved my Geri, and I'm going to take care of you."

"So, if I hadn't saved her, would you be putting me in the dumpster out back?" I asked as he led me to the sofa. My feet refused to lift all the way off the floor, and I had to shuffle along as he supported my weight with one arm around my waist.

He helped me onto the sofa, and I had to lie down. I couldn't even sit up anymore. As I did, Azriel gently pulled off my shoes and set them next to the leg of the sofa.

Azriel knelt next to the couch and stared into my eyes. "I would never hurt you. I'm in your debt forever for saving Tangerine, but even if you hadn't, I could never hurt you."

He brushed a lock of hair that had fallen over my forehead back behind my ear. A feeling like a warm blanket spread over me, but it came from inside. I couldn't tell if it was because of what he'd said to me or it was Meri's doing. My familiar had jumped up on the sofa and curled up next to me as a sleepiness like lead took hold.

I heard Azriel stand up and walk away from the sofa. I wanted to ask him to come back, but I couldn't keep myself awake. There was no choice but for me to drift off. I could no more

fight it than I could fight the sweeping powers
of a raging river.

The next thing I knew, Azriel's hand was on my shoulder shaking me gently. I almost brushed it away and told him I needed more sleep, but I smelled the intoxicating scent of garlic and cheese sauce.

"Fettuccine Alfredo from Bella Vita," he said as I pulled myself out of my stupor. "Garlic bread, toasted ravioli, and tiramisu too. I hope it's enough."

"How long have I been asleep?" I asked and sat up.

Azriel had cleaned up the pentagram, put the coffee table back, and laid the food out in a spread for me. In addition to the food, there was a huge plastic cup of Coke with a pink bendy straw sticking out of the top.

"Just twenty minutes. I made sure the man I sent knew there was a $1,000 bonus in it for him if he got back in under a half hour."

"You could have just ordered delivery. It would have cost you a lot less than a thousand dollars," I said and scooted to the edge of the sofa.

"It was worth it."

"I sort of knew that the garlic and vampire thing wasn't true, but I guess this proves it," I said.

"I rather like garlic," Azriel confirmed.

"Do you want some of this? I can share."

"That's sweet of you to offer, Kinsley, but no, thank you. Please, eat. If you want to be alone, I can go," he offered.

"It's your apartment," I said.

"I know I said I was calling in a favor, Kinsley, but I don't think you understand. When I said I was in your debt forever, I meant it. But, please eat. We can talk more when you're feeling better."

The food smelled so good, and my stomach felt like it was eating itself. So, I dug in. I ate it all. Every bite. If I hadn't had bread to mop up the sauce, I might have licked the container.

When the food was gone, I chugged the icy cold Coke like my life depended on it. "Let me clean this up," I said as I set the mostly empty cup back down on the coaster.

"You don't need to do that," he said. "You can rest some more, or I can take you home."

"I guess I should get out of here. I'm sure you have things you need to do."

"I won't be dealing with any more club business tonight. I plan to spend the rest of the evening here with Tangerine. You don't need to leave. If you want to stay for a while, that is."

I thought I might have detected a hint of anticipation in his voice, and I wasn't sure how to deal with it. Any other time, I would have reminded myself I was dating Thorn and left.

But something had shifted between me and Azriel. We'd bonded, and I knew then it wasn't something I could just deny.

"You'll take it the wrong way if I stay," I said.

"I won't take it any way, Kinsley," Azriel said. "You made it obvious to me before that you don't find me attractive. I'm not the type of man to beg for a woman's affection."

I opened my mouth to correct him, and then closed it again. He was wrong about me not finding him attractive, but what good would it do to correct him? Wouldn't I just be leading him on further? After all, I was dating Thorn and had been for some time. Things had been going well, and it seemed like we were getting serious. Still, it seemed rude to let him believe he wasn't attractive, and being around Azriel made me want to say and do stupid things.

"It's not that I don't find you attractive," I finally admitted. "I felt like I was already in a relationship with Thorn."

"And you don't now?" Azriel asked.

"I do. I mean, we've been dating for months."

"You just moved to town a few months ago. Didn't you just get divorced?" Azriel asked.

"Well, yes, but I'd been going through that divorce for a while," I said. "But I don't think I need to justify my decisions. Besides, you made a pass at me and we'd talked once."

"I wasn't trying to get into a relationship with you," Azriel said. "I was only interested in one thing."

"Wow," I said and felt my face grow hot with embarrassment. "I think maybe I should go home."

"I didn't mean to offend you, Kinsley. I'm only a man, and you're a beautiful woman," Azriel said. "But it's different now."

"That sounds like a line," I retorted.

"It's not."

I believed him for some reason. There was a sincerity in his eyes I could read from across the room. Plus, I could still feel his emotions, and he was telling the truth.

Suddenly, I was a mess of conflicted emotions. I didn't want to feel so drawn to him, and I certainly didn't want to have such a strong connection with someone other than Thorn. My love life had already been enough of a mess for two lifetimes. I had hoped that by spurning Azriel months ago, I would have avoided a love triangle. It seemed the universe had other plans. But what was this? A test to see if I truly wanted to be with Thorn? That seemed unfair.

"Has he told you that he loves you?" Azriel's stark question shocked me out of my internal reverie.

"What?"

"Has Thorn told you that he loves you?" he asked again, more slowly that time as if I hadn't understood him. I understood him fine. I just couldn't believe he was asking.

"What business is that of yours?" I countered.

"Well, answering a question with a question is a typical deflection move. I have a feeling that if the answer was *yes*, you'd have snapped something like *of course* at me."

"It's still none of your business," I said.

"How long have the two of you been together now?" Azriel asked.

I let out a deep, resigned sigh. He wasn't going to let up, so I figured I might as well answer. "It's been around six months," I said.

"And he hasn't told you that he loves you," he said flatly.

"Well, how long does it take you to tell a woman you love her?" I asked.

"I've never told a woman I loved her," Azriel said. "It would have been a lie. When I said that Tangerine was the only one who'd ever loved me, I meant it."

I stood there stunned for a moment, just biting my bottom lip. What was he getting at?

"Where are you going with this?" I asked.

"Do you love him?" he responded.

"Now you're answering a question with a question," I said.

"Just tell me this," Azriel said and took a step toward me. "Tell me you didn't feel that connection. Tell me that it was all in my head and that you weren't feeling my emotions and I wasn't feeling yours. Tell me that, and I will never bother you again. I swear it."

"I can't tell you that," I said after a few moment of weighing whether the situation called for the truth. He said he would leave me alone if I hadn't felt it. I could have lied and ended the entire thing right then and there. But, I couldn't do it. Because the truth was, as much as I cared about Thorn, I didn't love him. Yet. I had no idea if I ever would, but I'd never felt anything between him and me the way I felt with Azriel in those moments. "How do I know it's not just some trick you use to lure in prey?"

"Kinsley, you've been alone with me in my apartment for hours now. If I wanted to hurt you... If I even could hurt you... I would have done it by now. No one knows you're here."

"Meri knows I'm here," I said and looked over at my familiar.

"I'm sure he's a force to be reckoned with, but I've dealt with worse," Azriel said.

That was when I realized that Azriel didn't know that Meri was immortal. Meri couldn't die until the last of our family was dead, but Azriel had no idea. The fact that Meri could rat him out for hurting me wasn't the reason he hadn't tried because he didn't know that.

I was being super paranoid.

I could still feel Azriel's emotions, and he meant me no harm. It wasn't a trick or a trap unless he, a non-witch, was somehow overriding my intuition entirely. It was impossible. Azriel was as drawn to me as I was to him.

"I don't know what to do with this," I said.

Fortunately, or unfortunately depending on how you looked at it, neither one of us got to say another word. The sound of sirens approaching ended our little conversation on love and relationships.

"Stay here," Azriel said. "I leave them alone for a couple of hours..."

His voice trailed off as he walked toward the door. "Azriel?"

"Don't worry. I will take care of this."

The knowledge that Azriel was the leader of an outlaw biker club came roaring back. I'd nearly forgotten it watching him with Tangerine, and feeling the deep well of emotions inside of him, but he was technically a criminal.

My heart began to thunder in my chest, but not in a good way. I was terrified, but I wasn't sure of what. Maybe it was of him getting arrested. If whatever they did was bad enough, I might never see him again.

What if I got arrested for being there? I'd have to use my magic in a way I didn't believe in using it to spare my family. Could I use it to spare him? The thought of Azriel being ripped away from me before I could figure out the connection between us was almost unbearable in that moment. Again, the way I felt about him made me want to do stupid things.

I ran to him before he could open the door and threw my arms around him. I pressed my ear to his hard chest and listened for a heartbeat that I was surprised to find. He took a deep, shuddering breath and wrapped his arms around my shoulders.

"Please come back," I whispered. "Don't go away."

When I looked up at him, Azriel's eyes practically glowed with a feeling I didn't understand. Before I could pull away, his lips met mine. They were cold, but it wasn't unpleasant. We lingered that way for a few seconds, but then it had to end. I had to pull away. I didn't know if I wanted it to end, but I wasn't that kind of person.

"Your hair," he said and ran his hand over the back of my head.

I grabbed a lock and pulled it up so I could look at it. My hair had turned jet black. "It's black," I said bemused.

"It's beautiful," he said and kissed the top of my head. "I have to go. Stay here. I will come back."

Tangerine, who had settled down for a nap near the sofa, came to attention as Azriel began to open the door. He slipped out, though, before she could get up or I could say anything else.

"Your eyes are black too," Meri said once we were alone.

"No," I said and rushed down the hall to the bathroom.

He was right. My irises had turned very dark. They weren't entirely black. Up close, I could see that they were just a very, very dark purple.

But, from any kind of distance, they looked black. In the light over the bathroom mirror, my hair had a deep red sheen to it as well. Since my hair changed with my magic, I had to wonder what the colors meant. Black, red, and purple all had very specific meanings. It was some sort of weird mixture of royalty, love, and I was sure the black had to do with me using necromancy. It was a strange combination, to say the least.

"It's not so bad," Meri said. He must have sensed my distress. "I think your customers will eat it up."

"Thanks," I said.

"Whatever."

He sauntered out of the room and down the hall.

"What do we do now?" I asked as I followed.

"You think this guy has any bacon?"

"I doubt it. I'm sorry. I should have shared my dinner with you," I said. "Let me look in the pantry again. I swear I saw a can of something."

I went into the kitchen and opened the pantry door. Inside, I found a can sitting on the top shelf. I pulled it down and examined the label.

"What is it?" Meri asked eagerly from the kitchen.

"It's caviar. Do you like caviar?"

"What do you think?" he said and appeared in the pantry doorway.

"It looks expensive," I said.

"The guy said he owed you his life. I think he can spare a can of caviar for the familiar that helped save his dog."

"You're right," I said and popped the top of the can. "Here you go."

The sound of the can brought Tangerine running, but the two of them managed to share it without getting into any fights. When they were done, we all made our way into the living room. Tangerine resumed her nap, and I sat down on the edge of the sofa. Meri joined me, and I flipped on the television with the remote on the end table. It was on one of the news stations, but I didn't pay any attention. It was probably a weather forecast or something, but I was staring at the door.

It was as if I was trying to will Azriel to come back through it. I wanted to know he was all right, and I hated feeling trapped too.

Thorn was out there too. He had to be. I felt dreadful hiding inside, but what was I supposed to do? If I went outside just to assuage my guilt, I'd probably end up getting arrested. Things between Thorn and I would probably never be the same either. I wasn't ready to pull the pin on our relationship yet. Not over some shared feelings. It was all too fast.

I just wanted to go home and get some space from the situation. That was not what was going to happen.

The door opened, and I practically sprung off the sofa. Azriel came through first. "Kinsley, could you grab Tangerine? I don't want her to get out again."

Sure enough, she started to dart for the door, but Meri blocked her. I scooped her up and started toward the kitchen. That's when I saw Thorn and his deputies filing through the door.

Thorn saw me holding Azriel's dog. He heard him call out to me to grab her like us being alone in his apartment together was something we did all of the time.

The look on his face said it all. "I'm going to need you two to wait outside while we do the search," he said coldly.

"The search?" I said and handed Azriel the squirming Tangerine.

"They have probable cause to search my apartment. Come on," he said.

"You should listen to him," Thorn said curtly.

Azriel walked all the way to the edge of the lot and I followed. "What's going on?" I asked as soon as we were out of everyone's earshot.

"Someone called in a suspicious activity complaint," Azriel said. "When the sheriff got here, he and his men rolled up all quiet until they were practically in the lot. They turned on the lights and sirens and startled a few of my men that were doing some business outside. In the open. That gave your boyfriend probable cause to search the whole place."

"What are they going to find in your apartment?" I asked.

"Nothing," he said and smiled at me softly. "I'm not going anywhere tonight. Can't say the same for some of my men, but that's their own

61

stupid faults. I'll be able to get them out in a couple of days."

"Have you ever considered not being a criminal?" I asked.

"Not before tonight," he answered.

"Something changed tonight?" I asked, but I already knew what he was getting at.

"Yeah, you standing out here with me while they toss my apartment changes everything, Kinsley. I never want this to happen again. That gives me two options. One of them, I can't abide."

I didn't have to ask him what he meant. Either he stayed away from me completely, or he had to give up his *business*. Those were the only two options to ensure I never got wrapped up in something like that again. But what if I was the one that pulled the plug? I could tell him to leave me alone and never contact me again. We could pretend like what happened had never happened. I could just let it go.

Couldn't I?

"Don't even think about it," he said.

"How do you know what I'm thinking about?" I said. "We barely know each other."

"Don't," he said. "I've never had something like this with someone before. Please don't ruin it."

There was a pleading in his voice I hadn't expected. For just a moment, the tough exterior melted away again, and Azriel's vulnerability was laid bare for me.

"This is going to cause huge problems," I said. "I could already tell that Thorn was upset. Like, way beyond upset."

"He didn't even consider giving you the benefit of the doubt," Azriel said. "He just assumed you were up to no good. I could see it in his eyes. What does that say to you?"

"That's not fair," I said. "What would you have done in the same situation?"

"Probably take the other guy's head off," Azriel said with a shrug.

"You see. This is all going to be a problem."

The thing was, I had no idea. It was all about to get a lot worse than Thorn being upset and not trusting me.

63

When the whole search and arrest thing was over, Thorn didn't speak to me. He didn't even look at me. Since Azriel didn't get arrested, he took me home.

"I'm not going to disappear for months again," he said.

I just hugged him and went inside. It seemed like the thing to do. At that point, it was getting pretty late, so I put on my pajamas and went to bed.

When I got up the next morning, I made the executive decision to ignore everything that had happened. I was going to go to work, run my shop, and pretend like I hadn't become a necromancer with a disaster of a love life.

Neither my mother nor father texted me at any point, so I assumed that Thorn hadn't snitched on me. That made me feel a little bit better until I pulled up into the parking spot in front of my shop and saw that my windows were smashed in.

"What the... fluff?" I asked no one in particular as I got out of my car.

I looked around the square, and while there were people milling around doing what they were doing, no one was paying any attention to my smashed windows. I was about to yell something at all of them about how it was weird that no one had called the police when I noticed what looked like a wallet sitting in the middle of the smashed glass fragments on the sidewalk. That was enough of a distraction to keep me from losing my mind at everyone in the square.

Gingerly, I made my way over to the purple lump with a brass catch on the top. I probably should have called Thorn instead of just picking it up myself, but I wasn't thinking. I used my thumb and forefinger to twist open the little nubs that held the catch closed.

Inside the wallet was a stack of one- and five-dollar bills, two hair ties, a tube of lip balm, and a driver's license. I plucked out the driver's license and read the name. My breath caught in my throat, and I thought I might scream. A rage I hadn't known was even inside of me, that I was capable of, bubbled to the surface.

Without thinking, I slipped the license into the pocket of my jeans and snapped the wallet closed. I tried to breathe as I marched across the square toward Astra's shop. What I should have been doing was calling the sheriff, but I was blinded with rage. It was as if everything that had been piling up on me since my ex-husband had said he wanted a divorce had finally hit me. I'd been pushing through or leaning in since the start of my troubles, but in that moment, I was just... pissed off. At everything. And I didn't have myself collected by the time I got to Astra's shop.

My hand shot out in front of me and I pushed the door open with such force that it hit the stopper and almost bounced back and whacked me. I barely noticed as I barreled forward toward the cash register where she was standing there smiling at me. Ooh, that smile made me want to chuck the wallet at her.

"Good morning, Kinsley," she said in a singsongy voice that made steam come out of my ears. Not literally because that would have drawn way too much attention. I was doing that well enough without physical manifestations of my fury.

"What is the meaning of this?" I asked, holding up the wallet.

"Where did you get that?" Astra asked with a confused look on her face. It almost looked genuine. "How did you get my wallet?"

She reached for her purse, and I watched as she searched through it. When Astra got to the bottom, she set the purse back down on the counter behind her. She turned back around to face me, but I spoke before she had the chance.

"I found it in the glass on the sidewalk outside of my store. In case you don't know what I mean, and I highly doubt that, my shop windows are smashed in. Your wallet was lying in the middle of it all. Do you want to explain that?"

"What are you talking about? Are you nuts?" she spit.

"I'm not crazy, Astra. You destroyed my shop, but you made a mistake. You dropped your wallet. Probably while you were trying to get away."

"No, I didn't," she said. "I didn't smash your windows. I bet you stole my wallet. You knew your shop was going to fail, so you're setting me up. You probably smashed your own windows for the insurance money."

"That's... crazy! You did this!" I could feel my tether coming loose. I was about to actually go crazy. Not only did she destroy my store, but she was gaslighting me. "I told you not to mess with me, Astra Argent. You thought you'd get away with this, but you've made the biggest mistake of your life!"

And then Thorn's cruiser pulled up outside. No one had called the police about my windows being smashed, but me confronting Astra must have done the trick.

Thorn's face went from concerned to completely defeated when he saw it was me that was causing the "disturbance". For a split second, I felt bad, but then I got even angrier. He was making assumptions about me again. I could see it in the grimace he wore as he walked into Astra's shop. Not for one second did he even consider I might be in the right.

"What's going on here?" he asked Astra as he approached. He. Asked. Her.

It felt like my spine turned to cold steel when he ignored me. Clearly, he'd decided that she was the victim, and I was the criminal in the situation. Finding me at Azriel's had apparently tainted the way he saw me. On one hand, I could understand some of it. On the other, I was ticked that he'd lost faith in me so easily.

"Have you seen my shop?" I asked before Astra could say anything. I needed to get out ahead of this. "My windows are smashed. It's hilarious how no one has noticed. Oh, and I found this,"

I said and thrust the wallet toward him, "in the broken glass. It's her wallet. She must have dropped it when she was vandalizing the front of my store."

He took the wallet from me and looked it over. "This might have been evidence if you would have left it where you found it. Now, it can't be used because your prints are all over it."

"I..."

"How do you know it's Astra's wallet?" Thorn asked.

"I opened it and her driver's license was inside," I said. "Plus, I came here and she asked me how I got her wallet. So she admitted it was hers."

Thorn opened the catch and looked inside. "I don't see a driver's license."

"It's in my pocket," I said and pulled it out. "I don't know why I put it in there. I was upset, and I wasn't thinking."

He looked at me skeptically and then turned to Astra. "Is this your wallet?"

She thought it over for a moment. "I don't have any way of knowing for sure, but mine is missing. I certainly didn't smash her windows though. I swear. Kinsley said she was going to get revenge on me for daring to open a competing shop, but I didn't think she'd stoop to this."

"I didn't smash my own windows," I said.

"What other damage is there?" Thorn asked. "Is anything missing from the store?"

"I don't know," I admitted. "I didn't go inside and check. I was so upset, I came right here. Because I found the wallet. It was her."

"It's good that you didn't go inside, but you should have called right away instead of coming in here," Thorn said. "We'll deal with that later. Let's go see what other damage there is in your store."

"You're not going to arrest her for stealing my wallet?" Astra hissed.

"Ma'am, I'm going to investigate the damage to the store where your wallet was found. After I'm done with that, I will discuss your wallet with you," he said firmly.

It didn't entirely feel like he was on my side, but he definitely wasn't on hers. Perhaps I had read him wrong. It was entirely possible that he was disappointed but also worried about me.

"Why didn't you call me?" he asked as we crossed the street.

"Because she did this, and it got under my skin," I said. "I got angry, and I wasn't thinking straight."

"Does that have something to do with the new hair?" he asked softly. "Did you dye it that way for Azriel, or is there something deeper going on?"

I was taken aback by how calmly he'd just asked if I'd dyed my hair to please another man. We'd been dating for months, and he should have known me better than that. I could've given him the benefit of the doubt that he was still upset over the night before, but if that were the case, then he should have talked to me. Yeah, it was probably late when he got home, but I would've answered my phone.

"I can't believe you'd think I dyed my hair to please a man," I said.

"So it was magic that turned it that way," he whispered because there were people close by. "Magic that you did with Azriel Malum. What did he get you involved in?"

"What did he get me involved in?" I asked incredulously. "It's like you don't know me at all. You think a man is leading me around like I don't have a mind of my own?"

"I didn't say that," he countered.

"Yes, you did. That's pretty much what you said."

"So, can I ask why your hair is that color?"

"Of course you can ask," I said. "I'm not hiding anything from you."

But wasn't I? It's not like I was just coming out and telling Thorn that Azriel kissed me. I told myself it was because we needed to focus on the vandalism. I would tell him eventually. There was no way I'd lie to Thorn or withhold something like that. But, it needed to be the right time.

"They why were you at his place? Alone?" he asked through gritted teeth.

"We should talk about that," I said. "You should come over tonight and we can talk. It's not something I can just give you a five-second synopsis of."

"Just tell me this. Are you involved with him? Am I coming over tonight so you can break things off with me? Because I would have appreciated if you'd have told me that before you started seeing him."

"I'm not involved with Azriel," I said, and it was true. "That's not why I was there, and no, you're not coming over so I can break up with you. There's an entirely different reason I was there."

He seemed to relax a little. "How long have you been going over there and spending time alone with him?" he asked as we crossed the street to my shop.

"I haven't been, Thorn. I went over there last night to help him with something. It was magic related. He called in his favor last night, and it was a spell. That's it."

That really wasn't it, but I hadn't made heads or tails of what happened between Azriel and me. How could I possibly explain it to Thorn? I had to get my head around it, and then I could talk it out with him. I planned to do exactly that once the vandalism stuff was handled. I told myself that I'd do the police report, call the insurance company, schedule the glass repair, and then I'd spend the afternoon figuring out what was next for me.

"You're not involved with him?"

"I already said I'm not."

"But whatever you did with him turned your hair black."

"I have an explanation for that," I said. "And it doesn't involve me cheating on you."

Ugh, the feeling of just oily nastiness came over me. Azriel had kissed me, and I hadn't kissed him back, but it still felt like lying.

By that point, we were standing at the edge of the broken glass. It would have to wait.

"I think the shadow of the buildings is why no one noticed and called," Thorn said. His voice pulled me out of my thoughts.

"What?"

"Your store was in the shadow of the buildings this morning. I think that's why no one noticed," he said.

I walked back across the street to the square. He was right. Without the sun shining on the glass, it was easy to miss. Especially since no one was really on my side of the square yet. Most of the shops on that side were just getting ready to open.

"Maybe it's that," I said. "Or maybe Astra cast a spell to keep people from noticing."

That part I said when I was already back across the street and standing right next to him. The fresh scent of his laundry soap mixed with his aftershave hit me, and it took all of my strength not to wrap my arms around him. Whatever had happened when I was near Azriel faded away, and Thorn felt like home again. A home I was probably going to lose because I'd been stupid.

"We should go inside and see if there is anything missing," Thorn said. His words weren't as harsh as they were before, and the look in his eyes had softened.

"Okay."

"I'll go in first," he said. "I doubt they are still in there, but just in case, you stay behind me."

Fortunately, whoever smashed the windows, and I still knew it was Astra, hadn't wrecked my entire shop. There was glass everywhere, but they hadn't damaged my shelves or my stock. It wasn't until we reached the stock room that I found what was missing.

The vandal was actually a thief. What they had stolen was all of the swag bags we'd put together for the Midnight Magic Festival and all of the decorations I'd made. The festival was days away and it was all gone.

"What is it?" Thorn asked, and I realized I was crying.

"She took all of the bags I put together for the festival. All of the decorations are gone too. People are going to be so disappointed, and I'm going to look like a fool," I said with a sniffle. "I can't believe this is happening."

But I could believe it. I felt like I was being punished for using necromancy, but I'd done it for good. I wasn't trying to be evil, and I hadn't done it for personal gain either.

He pulled me in for a hug, and for a moment, I felt better. Then my guilt overwhelmed me. "He kissed me, Thorn," I said and felt him stiffen. "Last night, Azriel kissed me. That's not why I was there, though. It wasn't a date or anything like that. It just... happened. I know that sounds so bad."

He held me at arm's length, but Thorn didn't entirely let me go. "Is that? Is that as far as it went?"

"Yeah. It was just a weird confusing thing that happened. I have this connection to him."

That was enough to get him to let me go. "You have a connection to him?"

"It's like an empathic connection. I discovered it last night for the first time. I was there trying to save his dog," I said. "It's a long story."

"I need to start the report for the burglary," he said and turned to walk away from me.

"Thorn..." I called after him as he walked toward the door.

"Not right now," he said without stopping. "You said we could discuss it tonight, and I think that's best."

At least he was still going to talk to me. I took that as a good sign. The night before, I hadn't been sure if I loved Thorn, but I knew right then I was terrified of losing him. I would not have handled it well if he'd never spoken to me again.

Chapter Three

 While I was waiting for a man to come from a glass shop a few towns over to give me an estimate on the windows, I decided to go get a coffee and talk to Viv.

"Whoa. You look terrible," she said as I stepped up to the counter.

"That's because the windows to my shop got smashed into oblivion and whoever did it stole all of my bags for the festival. The decorations I made too."

"What?" Viv asked.

"Yeah. Anyway, I need a bucket of hazelnut latte," I said. "Also, did you not see the smashed glass all over the sidewalk when you opened this morning? It's just so weird to me that nobody called the sheriff."

"I parked in the back and came in through the kitchen door this morning, hon. I do most mornings. I didn't see anything when I opened this morning, but I wasn't really looking either," she said with a frown. "I'm so sorry. You know I would have called Thorn and you if I had."

"Has business been slow this morning?" I asked. "Again, it's just so weird to me that nobody saw it."

"Now that you mention it, it has been kind of a slow morning. I wonder if any of the tourists saw it and didn't call it in," Viv said as she went to work making the espresso for my latte. "Maybe they figured it was already handled or that it was none of their business. You know how people can be. Most of the people who work at the courthouse go in through the back too, and hardly anyone uses the library anymore."

"You're right," I said. "But I haven't told you the best part. I found Astra's wallet in the smashed glass."

"No, you didn't!" Viv made half her customers jump when she hollered. "Sorry, folks. Just had a little too much of my dark brew this morning."

"Yeah, she did it. I know she did. I had evidence," I said.

"Did Thorn arrest her?"

"No," I said. "Get this, she said I stole her wallet. He did a report, but he said there wasn't enough evidence to arrest either of us."

"Wait, he considered arresting you? He believed her?" Viv asked.

"Yeah." I didn't elaborate further.

"You guys on the rocks?"

"I guess we are," I said. "It's a long story."

"You can tell me while we're cleaning up the mess," she said.

But I couldn't. I couldn't tell her the real reason I was over at Azriel's place. I couldn't tell her what I had done for him. I'd have to find a cover story, but nothing I came up with was going to make any sense.

"I've got someone coming in to clean it up," I said. "But thank you for the offer."

It was a lie, but I couldn't tell her the truth about the cleanup either. I'd sweep the glass out front up by hand, but inside, I was going to use magic. I estimated I'd be done with the whole thing within an hour.

I just had to wait for the glass guy to come give his estimate. Castor was going to pay him with cash because he didn't want a claim on his insurance.

"Well, you call me if you need me," she said and handed me my finished latte. "Actually, call me later anyway."

"I will."

We said our goodbyes, and I walked back over to my shop to begin the process of sweeping up the glass. Some days Meri stayed home because he thought the shop was boring, and that day I wished he was there.

Five minutes later as I was sweeping up glass fragments, Meri came galloping down the sidewalk. He plopped down on the sidewalk next to where I'd set my coffee and watched me sweep with a soft expression.

As I was sweeping up the last dustpan of glass, a truck with a sign that said Hartman's Glass pulled up in front of the shop. A couple of women approached the store from the square, but when they saw the broken windows, they hurried on.

The man in the truck got out and grabbed a small box from the bed of the truck. He was a burly guy dressed in a plaid flannel shirt and loose khaki cargo pants. His face was broad with a beard that was somewhere between "forgot to shave for three days" and an actual beard. While he looked to be in his late forties or early fifties, he had bright hazel eyes that looked far younger.

"Hello, ma'am," he called out cheerfully. "You Kinsley?"

"I am," I said. "You're Dennis, right?"

"That's me," he said and then looked at the broken front windows. He let out a long whistle. "This is going to cost a pretty penny. Castor's lucky he and I are friends."

Dennis chuckled. He set his box down on the sidewalk and pulled out a huge measuring tape and tiny notebook.

"I'm guessing they are expensive because I'll need custom panes?" I asked. "How long does that take?"

"It's going to take up to eight weeks for tempered glass replacement windows," he said and I felt my stomach churn.

"Eight weeks..." I swallowed the lump in my throat.

"Don't worry, Kinsley. I'll go back to my shop and cut some laminate panes this afternoon. It's only a temporary fix, but unless there's a huge storm or something, they'll hold until I get done with the glass. I can come back tomorrow and put them in. I've got some plastic sheeting in the truck I'll put over it for now."

"Really?"

"Yes, ma'am," he said with a smile. "But the plastic sheeting won't keep thieves out. Just the elements."

"Don't worry about that. I'll take care of all of that."

I hadn't really thought about how I would take care of all of that. I'd have to use magic, of course. I cursed myself for not having protection wards up around the store in the first place. Because I hadn't wanted to use spells, Castor was going to have to pay money for the repairs. I wouldn't make that mistake again. Protecting myself and my shop was a good enough reason to use magic.

Once Dennis was done measuring, he got huge sheets of plastic out of the bed of his truck. I watched quietly as he hung them. It was obviously something he was well practiced at. It seemed like it took him no time at all to cover the huge front store windows.

"Did you get that coffee across the square over there?" Dennis asked as he packed notebook and measuring tape back into his little toolbox.

"I did. Viv makes a great cup of joe," I said.

"I smelled the place as I drove by. I think I'm going to mosey on over there," he said.

"Well, tell Viv I sent you, and she'll give you your first cup for free," I said. "But tomorrow, you'll have to pay. It'll get you hooked."

"I'm not one to pass up a free cup of coffee." Dennis put his toolbox back in the bed of his truck. "I'll see you tomorrow about this time to put up the temporary windows?"

"Thank you so much, Dennis."

"You're welcome, Kinsley."

He put his ladder away last, and then headed across the square to grab his coffee. I went inside the shop and magically directed all of the glass scattered around into a garbage can.

When that was done, I drew sigils on the doorframes with ink that turned invisible with a snap of my fingers. Astra Argent would never set foot in my store again.

I debated whether or not to open the store, but it didn't seem like there was much point. Who was going to come in with the giant plastic sheets hanging over the windows?

It was just one day, and I figured it wouldn't hurt to stay closed until Dennis came back and put up the temporary windows.

"What are you going to do?" Meri asked as I stood there staring at the front of the store.

"Let's go home. I can get on the internet and see if there's any way to replace what was stolen in time," I said.

"You're going to buy it all again?" Meri asked. "I thought Thorn was going to try to get a search warrant for Astra's place?"

He was, but I didn't have much faith in it. He hadn't sounded confident he'd get one, and I wasn't even sure how hard he would try.

But, I had another idea forming in the back of my mind.

"It's just in case," I said. "I think I might have another idea."

"What is it?" Meri asked enthusiastically. I think he'd picked up on the fact that I was locked, loaded, and ready for some mischief.

"I'll tell you on the way home."

My grand idea was that I'd go to Astra's shop in the middle of the night and do a little breaking and entering. If I found my swag bags and decorations, I'd just steal them back. What could she do? Call the sheriff and tell him I'd stolen what she'd stolen from me? The idea was laughable.

"What if you get caught?" Meri asked as we went inside the house.

"We're not going to let that happen," I said.

"Oh, you think I'm getting involved in this drama?"

"Well, yeah. It's your job to protect me."

"Maybe you should just wait for the search warrant," Meri suggested.

"That sounds lame," I said. "Are you going soft on me?"

"Whatever." Meri said. "Sure, let's go do a burglary later, but I want extra bacon."

The rest of the day, I spent shopping online for replacements for the swag and decorations. I didn't buy any of it because I hoped to get what I'd already done back. Plus, it would cost me hundreds of dollars in rush delivery fees to get things in time.

Late in the afternoon, I got a text from Thorn. He said he would be over later, but that he wouldn't be in time for dinner.

My stomach growled because I'd forgotten to have lunch. I figured if he wasn't coming for dinner, I'd just head over to the diner and have an early dinner or late lunch. Maybe I'd eat enough for both.

I grabbed some cash and stuffed it into my purse. "I'm going to the diner to get food. I'll bring you back bacon," I called out to Meri.

"Thanks, Creature," he said.

It had been a long while since he called me that. I felt myself choke up a little, but I was too hungry to dwell.

I drove over to the diner and found the parking lot mostly empty. Reggie was inside at the counter rolling silverware up in napkins. She looked up and smiled as I came through the main entrance.

"Hey, I wasn't expecting to see you today," she said and came out from behind the counter. "Sit anywhere you like. I'm the only one here until Leslie comes in for the dinner shift."

"Do you have to work tonight too?" I asked as I took a seat at the counter.

Reggie plopped down on the stool next to me. "No. Amanda's on tonight too. Her rent is due in two days, so she'll be in no matter what. When she's worried about getting evicted is the only time I can count on her, though."

"Have you ever thought about doing something other than this?" I asked as I looked over the menu.

"Like what?" Reggie asked and pulled the tub of silverware and pile of napkins over so she could keep rolling. "I have like three credits of community college and the only other work experience I have is two days of complete failure working as a secretary at the hospital. That did not go well. It's too bad too because the pay was good and there was insurance."

"I was thinking of hiring someone at the shop, you know," I said.

"And?" she asked.

"Oh my gawd, Reggie. I'm trying to ask if you're interested," I said and playfully punched her arm. "Of course, you'll have to wait until tomorrow to start. I'm obviously not open today."

"Why aren't you at work?" she asked instead of answering me.

"I can't believe you haven't heard. Someone smashed the front windows out of my shop and stole all of my swag bags and decorations for the Midnight Magic Festival."

"I heard there was some sort of ruckus downtown, but we've hardly had any customers today. So the gossip train didn't pull into this station today. Do you know who did it?"

"That's the craziest part. I found Astra Argent's wallet at the scene."

"No way. That crazy... woman. Did Thorn arrest her?"

"She accused me of stealing the wallet. He said there wasn't enough evidence to arrest either of us, so he's going to try to get a search warrant for her place," I said.

"That's nuts. How can that not be enough evidence to arrest her? You found her wallet there. I'd assume she dropped it."

"Because I didn't leave it there. I wasn't thinking, and I picked it up. I took it with me when I went over to confront her."

"Oops. Still, I can't believe Thorn didn't arrest her. Are you guys doing okay?"

"I think he's just stressed from working so many hours. He really needs to hire another deputy," I said. I was going to tell her why Thorn was really upset with me. If she was going to work with me in the shop, I might as well come clean about who I really was, but I wasn't going to tell her about it in the diner.

"Any idea what you want to eat?" she asked.

"Chicken strips and waffles with a triple side of bacon," I said.

"You want one of those sides of bacon to go?"

"You know it," I said.

"Honey mustard for the chicken and blueberry syrup for the waffles?" Reggie asked.

"This place is going to miss you," I said.

"How do you know I'm going to come work for you?"

"Because I'm going to pay you a decent wage and get you health insurance," I said.

"What about my grandmother?" Reggie said. "Sure would be nice to get her off the state health insurance."

"You've got a deal."

"Really? You'd really do that? I was just joking around. Kinsley, you can't. It will be so expensive."

"Then I guess you'd better say yes."

"Oh my gawd, girl. Yes, of course. And I can start tomorrow?"

"Yeah, it might take me a few days to get the insurance in place, but I know someone who can probably hook me up. I've still got one or two friends left in the city who didn't completely jump ship on me after the divorce. We can join a group co-op thingy."

"You, my dear, are a rock star. And to do that for me when you've got your own stuff going on."

"They say the best way to feel better about your problems is to help someone else with theirs."

"This is so great," Reggie said. "Let me go put your order in."

When she got back, Reggie plopped back down next to me and started rolling silverware again. "What are they going to do tomorrow without you?" I asked. "Should I let you give them longer notice?"

"Nah. The manager will just have to work for a few days until they move someone to the day shift or hire someone else. It'll do her good to actually do some work."

"Are you sure?"

"Yeah, I'm done here. I was so hoping you ask me to work with you when you started talking about needing an assistant," Reggie said.

"Why didn't you just ask me?"

"I figured if you wanted me to work with you, you'd ask. And, you did," she said and threw her arms around my shoulders.

A few minute later, my food was ready and a handful of people moseyed in for an early dinner. I was hanging around waiting to see if Reggie got another break in the action when I got a text from Thorn.

It's quiet right now. Meet me at the spot?

The spot was a bench by the new pond in the cemetery. It was a tranquil place to get some sunshine and fresh air. It was also neutral ground for us to talk.

I'll be there in a few. I texted back.

He didn't say anything else, so I left money for my check. "I'll call you later," I told Reggie on my way out.

I was at the cemetery for around half an hour before Thorn showed up. It gave me time to go over what I was going to say in my head. Not that it helped.

My stomach started doing flip-flops as I watched his cruiser get closer. I wasn't sure why, but I had a bad feeling.

When he parked the car across the little grave road from the pond, I watched Thorn as he sat there for a full minute looking at me. Finally, he let out a big sigh and got out of the car.

He put his hat on the driver's seat and closed the door before making his way over to the bench and sitting down next to me. "I came here to break things off with you," he said grimly.

It felt like someone had punched me in the chest. I had to take a deep breath past the lump in my throat to keep from throwing up. My face grew hot and my mouth started to tingle that way it does right before you get sick.

I must have sounded like I was struggling to breathe, but that's because I was. If a person could look furious and concerned at the same time, that's exactly how Thorn looked.

He put a hand on my knee. "But I can't do it, Kinsley. Seeing you sitting here, I realized how foolish I was being."

"So, you're not breaking up with me?" I managed to say.

"Not unless that's what you want," he said. "I'm not happy about anything that's happened in the last couple of days, but I can't just let you go. I care about you too much. In fact, I think that I might even love you."

"Thorn..."

"Now, I know it's a really awkward time for me to say something like that, so please don't say it back. But maybe if I'd told you that before, none of this would be happening. I'll carry that responsibility."

"You're not responsible for the things I do," I said.

"I kind of am, Kinsley. I should have been more open with you, and I wish that I could promise that I will be. I don't know if I can make that promise right now, but if you want to work things out, I think we can get through this."

"I do want to work things out," I said. "I'm sorry about all of this, and I'm sorry I didn't tell you what happened right away."

"Part of me can understand why you didn't," he said and rubbed his chin. For the first time I noticed how exhausted he looked. Thorn had been tired lately, but that day he looked like he was at the very end of a short tether. "But if you still want to be with me while you have this connection or whatever to Azriel Malum, then you're going to need to promise me that you'll never see him again. No more favors. No more magical spells to help him out. You've got to cut him off and never look back."

I knew what Thorn was saying was the truth, but at the same time, it felt like he'd punched me in the chest all over again. Like, the idea of never seeing Azriel again, even as a friend, nearly knocked the wind out of me. I held it together, though. After all, I had a history with Thorn. It wasn't like I could just throw that away because I'd discovered some weird empathic connection to Azriel.

"Can you do that?" he asked.

Before I could answer, his radio squawked to life. I was about to say something, but I wasn't sure what. I guess I hoped I'd open my mouth and the right thing would come out.

"I'll come over later. I should be able to get away once most of the good folks of Coventry are settled in for the night," Thorn said. "It will be after dinnertime, but it shouldn't be too late."

"Okay," I said. "I'll see you then."

He leaned over and gave me a quick kiss on the lips before hurrying back to his cruiser. I sat there staring at the water lapping against the bank of the pond for a while. I felt stunned.

My whole life had been turned upside down by my divorce and then I had nearly six months of peace. Once again, it had been turned upside down. The chaos in me could be wielded as a great power, but it also seeped into my everyday life. I wondered if I'd ever have any peace long-term, but then I decided not to dwell on that.

I sat there for a long time just trying not to think. I had bacon for Meri, and I could have gone home to give it to him, but it felt like if I moved from that spot, it would all come crashing down. Thorn had asked me to meet him there so he could break things off with me, but then he hadn't. I felt a familiar lump rise in my throat. My eyes got misty, and I was about to cry when I got a text message.

Come see me. It was from Azriel.

I don't know if this is a good time.

I texted back still not sure if I even wanted to get off the bench. My body felt so heavy. You'd have thought I would have been happy that Thorn decided not to dump me, but I was still so full of grief.

Whatever it is, I can help. Come see me. Or just tell me where you are. I'll come to you. he responded.

He could feel my sadness. It was a little weird knowing that I wasn't really alone, but also sort of comforting. I'd assumed the connection only worked when we were close, but perhaps it stretched further when the emotions were more intense. Or perhaps now that we'd discovered it, the actual connection grew stronger.

I hadn't promised Thorn I wouldn't see Azriel again because I hadn't had the chance. Given what had transpired between us, I thought it was better if I told him in person anyway. I didn't owe him a face-to-face talk, but it felt like I did.

I'll come to you. I answered.

With that, I was finally able to move. Just enough of the heaviness inside of me lifted, and I got myself up and off the bench. He was literally the only person I could talk to about this. Other than Meri, and I knew how that would go. I could have also gone to my Mom and Dad, but that felt weird. Lilith would tell me that if I had that kind of connection with Azriel, I should go with it. I could almost hear her saying to "ditch that square sheriff".

But Thorn had said that he loved me, and that meant something. So, I had to tell Azriel that I couldn't see him again. There would be no relationship or friendship. The weird anomaly between us was something for us to ignore, not to embrace.

I got in my car and drove to the clubhouse. After parking my car around back, I made my way up the concrete steps and across the loading dock. I tried to ignore the memories of the night before. I refused to feel the pulse of power through my veins as I embraced the dark arts and brought his dog back to life.

As I lifted my hand to knock on the door, it opened. He'd been waiting for me.

"I have more wine," Azriel said as he stepped back and let me enter.

"It's not even dinnertime," I said. "I'm not sure I should have a glass so early."

"It's late enough," he countered. "I promise I won't let you have too much."

"Like I need you to look after me," I teased.

"Glad to know you're feeling better," he said as we walked into the kitchen.

And I was. I'd even begun bantering with him without realizing it. I needed to tone it down a notch since I was there to deliver bad news. It was just that as soon as I was around Azriel, I forgot myself.

"Speaking of feeling better, how is Tangerine?" I changed the subject. It seemed the safest thing to do.

"For a zombie dog, she's pretty great," he said with a smile.

"Oh, no. Why did you call her a zombie dog? Is something... decaying?"

He laughed at that and grabbed a bottle of white wine from his refrigerator. "Something light for the late afternoon?"

In his hand was a bottle of pink Moscato. "That sounds great. I didn't see that in there the other day."

"Just something I picked up in case I had company," he said and went to work removing the cork. "Anyway, to answer your question, no. There's nothing actually zombie-like about Tangerine. That was a joke because you brought her back from the dead. You'd never know she was brought back from the other side."

"Oh, good," I said and he handed me the glass of pink wine.

"Let's go sit down," he said and walked into the living room.

I followed behind him and sat down on the sofa I'd napped on the evening before. I'd thought that Azriel would take a seat in one of the chairs flanking the sofa, but he sat down next to me. Still, there was enough space between us that it felt friendly.

"This is good," I said as I took a small sip of the wine. I'd have to be careful with it as it was sweet and went down way too easily.

"So, tell me what's going on," Azriel said.

And I did.

When I was done telling him about the day, his eyes were even softer than before. He looked at me with a concern I hadn't expected, but there wasn't a trace of pity on his face.

"I can't believe he told you that he was going to break it off with you," Azriel said when he finally spoke. "I can't believe he told you that even after he changed his mind."

"What do you mean?"

"It just seems so cruel. If he'd changed his mind, then why not keep that to himself? Why put you through that pain?"

"I don't know," I said and bit my bottom lip. "I hadn't thought of it that way. I guess that's why I didn't feel any relief."

"So, you promised him you'd never see me again?" Azriel asked and reached out his hand for my wine glass. I handed it to him, and he took a drink. "But you're here."

"I didn't promise him. He got a call on the radio before I could say anything," I said.

"You're here to tell me in person that you're never going to see me again," he said and handed the glass back to me. "You wanted to do it face to face. You're a good person like that."

I thought about what he'd said. How it was cruel for Thorn to tell me that he'd planned on breaking up with me even though he'd changed his mind. I didn't know if I'd changed my mind because I didn't know what to think, but I wasn't going to tell him that I'd come there to do that.

"I'm here because you're the only person I could talk to about this." It was the truth.

He visibly relaxed. Azriel had been waiting for me to tell him I was never going to see him again.

"I know we barely know each other, Kinsley, but I don't think this connection is for nothing. I've been around long enough to know that these things happen for a reason. Hell, I don't even believe in coincidences anymore."

"I don't know what to do," I said. "I have no idea how to process any of this, and with the break-in this morning, my whole life is upside down. It doesn't feel like I'm ever going to find any peace."

"I will find out who did that to your shop, Kinsley," he said.

"I'm not sure if it's a good idea for me to owe you any more favors," I said with a chuckle. "The last one had me raising the dead."

"I know that you're kidding," he said and took my hand, "but just in case there is any part of you that's worried about owing me anything, don't. I told you that I'm in your debt. Even if you never spoke to me again, I'd still be here waiting for you. Anything you ever needed. If I could get it for you, I would."

I felt my heart start to hammer in my chest. Azriel was just so... unexpected. Being there with him, I felt better. I wanted to hate myself for it, but I did feel better.

"Can I tell you something?"

"Anything," he said and squeezed my hand.

"Since I think that.... since I know that Astra did this, I was considering breaking into her shop tonight to see if she had my stuff there. Thorn said he'd try to get a search warrant, but he didn't sound confident. I figured I could steal my stuff back, and what can she do?"

He let go of my hand and rubbed his palms together. "I know I shouldn't be encouraging this, but it sounds like a good time to me."

I couldn't help but laugh a little. "I thought you'd said you were considering abandoning your life of crime?"

"This isn't crime. It's vigilante justice. Besides, I just said I was considering abandoning my criminal enterprises. It's a lot more complicated than just walking away."

"Is it though?" I asked and for the first time, I found myself wondering what the "outlaw" part of his biker club entailed. I knew I probably shouldn't ask, but it slipped out before my brain could catch up with my mouth. "What is it you guys do anyway?"

"I don't want to lie to you, Kinsley, so let's just say we don't hurt women and children and leave it at that, okay? It's better for you that way."

"What about drugs?"

"If we were involved in that business, and I'm not saying one way or another, it wouldn't be with the stuff that kills people," he said.

I took a deep breath. "Okay, I'll leave it alone."

"Look, this isn't easy for me either. I never expected to care about anyone, let alone someone like you. My whole life is turned upside down too."

"What are we going to do?"

"Tonight we're going to break into Astra's store and find your stuff," he said. "Let's focus on things where we can take action."

"And if it's not there?"

"Then we'll go to her house. Or I'll send some of my men to her house," Azriel said.

"I don't want them to hurt her," I said. "I mean, I do... kinda... but it wouldn't be right."

"We can search her house without hurting her, Kinsley. This is what we do. We're professionals."

"Let's just start with her shop. It would have been much easier for her to get it there than to take it all the way home."

"What do you think her plan was?" Azriel asked. "Why did she do this?"

"I think just to make me look bad," I said. "It's not like she can give out the bags or even sell the stuff in them. She'd probably have to throw it all away. I'm convinced it was all just to make me look bad."

"Do you think she's just a nasty person? Why would she do this to you."

"I think you hit the nail on the head. I never met her before she moved to town. It's not like we had a feud going on or something."

And that's when it hit me. What if she was a Tuttlesmith witch and had no idea that I was one as well? My last name was Skeenbauer, but maybe Astra didn't know my mother was a Tuttlesmith.

"Well, she'll be dealt with," Azriel said.

"You sound like you intend to kill her."

"No, not that. But I've run my share of nasty... problems out of town," he said.

"I can imagine," I said. "If you have things you need to do, I can go."

"Kinsley, if I didn't have time for you, I wouldn't have invited you over," he said. "I was thinking about watching a movie, though. That new movie with the arsonist that gets caught in a haunted house is out on demand. You're welcome to stay and watch it with me. You could have another glass of wine, and I was going to make some Parmesan and red pepper popcorn."

"Not too much red pepper?" I said hopefully.

"Just enough for a kick. Not enough to set your mouth on fire. I'll let you control it if you'd like."

"I'd like to see the movie," I said.

"I know it's more than a decision to stay and watch the movie, Kinsley," Azriel said. "I know it potentially means letting Thorn go, and you're not ready to make that decision. I'm not here to force you into choosing anything. I won't be mad if you go."

"It is just a movie," I said. "I think I'll stay and watch it. Let's make the popcorn, and do you have a Coke? I don't want to drink too much wine."

I wasn't ready to just dump Thorn, but I didn't like being backed into a corner either. What if I did want to be friends with Azriel? Was it Thorn's place to tell me that couldn't happen?

Whatever the outcome, I just wanted to let it go for a while. I'd talk to Thorn later, and perhaps we could handle the whole thing a little less dramatically.

Chapter Four

By the time the movie was over, it was getting close to seven. "I need to head out," I said. "Thorn is supposed to come over after work, and I think we have a lot of talking to do."

"I understand," he said and kissed the top of my head. "I'm here for you if you need me. No matter how late."

"Thank you," I said and left before I could get emotional all over again.

I drove home, trying to figure out what I was going to say. That wasn't exactly easy because I still didn't know what I wanted. What I wanted was time to sort things out, but Thorn wanted reassurances. I wasn't sure if that was something I had to offer him, but I didn't want to drive him away either. We'd talked every day for almost six months. If he completely turned his back on me, it felt like I'd have a huge hole in my life.

When I turned onto my street, I noticed someone sitting on my front porch. At first, I thought Thorn had shown up earlier than I expected and he was waiting for me. But neither his cruiser nor his truck was in my driveway.

As I got closer, I recognized it was Astra. Had she come to pick a fight? Was she there to confess and make things right by giving my bags and decorations back?

There wasn't a car in my driveway from what I could see, so either she'd pulled up really far, walked, or someone had dropped her off. When I pulled into the driveway, I saw that there was no car at all.

She was just sitting there on the porch with some sort of tropical-looking drink in her hand, staring at me with this creepy smile. It was unnerving, to say the least.

What was even worse was how fixated on me her glare was. She wasn't moving at all.

"What are you doing here?" I asked as I got out of the car.

Just then, Meri jumped into the window behind her. He was pawing at the glass frantically. "Let me out," I heard him call.

"What is wrong with you?" I asked as I walked up the steps.

What was wrong with him was that Astra wasn't glaring at me without moving. She wasn't moving because she was dead.

Not sure exactly what to do, I unlocked the door quickly and let Meri out. "Are you okay?" I asked. "Was someone in there with you?"

"No, no one's in the house," he said and ran over to me.

I scooped him up and held him against my chest. "Who did this?" I asked. "Did you see who did this?"

"No. I looked out the window a while back and she was there. I didn't see anybody. I might have heard a car at some point, but I was up in the attic. When it wasn't you, I just sort of went back to what I was doing."

"I need to call Thorn," I said and carried Meri down the steps.

We stood in the middle of the yard, and I took out my phone. My front porch was a crime scene, and I wanted to avoid contaminating it any more than I already had.

"I'll be about another half an hour," Thorn said when he picked up.

"I'm not calling because of that," I said, and then I told him what I found.

Meri and I waited there in the middle of the yard until he and a couple of his deputies arrived. They took pictures and collected fingerprints. Thorn made the decision not to call in crime scene techs because there wasn't any other evidence to collect. However she died, it hadn't left any blood or other such evidence. He did call the coroner and came over to take my statement while we waited.

"Did you kill her?" he asked first off.

"What?"

"Are you really saying that someone killed her on your porch or brought her body here and staged it, and you didn't hear anything. You had no idea what was going on outside of your window?"

"I wasn't here," I said. "I just got home, and I found her that way."

"You were still in the cemetery?" he asked. "You stayed there all that time?"

Well, there wasn't any way around it. I was going to have to tell him where I'd been. If nothing else, Azriel was my alibi. He could vouch for my whereabouts, and at least I wouldn't be a suspect.

"Okay, I don't know any way to say this other than to just come out with it. I was with Azriel," I said.

A coldness I hadn't expected chilled his blue eyes. "You went to see him after our talk? Why, Kinsley?"

"I went to go talk to him about what you'd said, and I ended up staying to watch a movie."

"You did what?" he asked and then I watched his entire demeanor change. "You know what, I don't have time for this right now. I'm going to take your statement, and I'll check your alibi with Mr. Malum. Assuming it checks out, I will let you know if I have any further questions for you. So please, go over your discovery of the body one more time for me."

It was all business after that. My Mom and Dad did show up a little while later when it got back to them what had happened. I sat in their car while I waited for the coroner to release the scene.

"I don't think you should beat yourself up over this," Mom finally said.

"Over Astra's death?" I asked.

"Over the prickly situation with Thorn," she responded.

"You know about that?"

"There's not much that goes on in this town I don't know about," she said. "Even when it comes to Azriel Malum."

"Oh," I said.

"We're not going to judge you, honey," my dad said.

"Thorn is a nice guy," Mom said. "His father did the best he could with him, and he's a good friend of the family."

"But?" I asked. "I sense there's a but here."

"Well, Thorn Sr. wasn't exactly known for sticking around. And, that's okay. Everything worked out for the best, but he had a tendency to run from things. The only exception was his ex-wife, and that's a dynamic that I don't really need to get into," she said.

"Yeah, from what little you've told me over the years, it seemed like a bad situation."

"It was," Mom said. "So Thorn Jr. may not have had the best role model when it came to healthy relationships."

"Well, I did, and look how I turned out anyway," I said.

"Two things on that," Dad said. "One is that your mother is amazing, but I've had my issues with... the darkness in the past. It's gotten its claws into me and made me do things I wasn't proud of. This was way before you were born, but your mother handled it better than I deserved."

"What did you do?" I couldn't believe what I was hearing.

"I messed around with some dark magic I had no business in and it turned me a little obsessive. I was a bit stalkery for a while."

"What?"

"In all fairness, your dad was trying to do the right thing. He just managed to go about it all wrong. It was a mess, but it was a mess I understood and forgave because he's my soulmate," Mom said. "People aren't perfect, Kinsley. Sometimes they get mixed up in things they shouldn't, but that doesn't mean you can't forgive them. It doesn't mean they can't change."

I got the feeling she was talking more about Azriel than about Thorn, but I was too afraid or too emotionally exhausted to ask. "You said there were two things about Thorn?"

My Dad let out a deep breath through his nose. "I don't even like to bring it up because it's probably not fair, but you're my daughter. Things don't have to be fair when it comes to me protecting you."

"Protecting me? From Thorn?"

"It might be nothing," Mom said.

"But there's always the chance that it is," Dad said. "What we're getting at is that Thorn Jr.'s biological father could be Thorn Sr.'s brother. He's the man that broke up Thorn Sr.'s marriage the first time around. That would most likely explain why Thorn. Jr. looks so much like his dad even though he's not his biological father."

"So he's his uncle. Okay?" I was confused.

"Thorn Sr.'s brother wasn't a good man," Mom said. "In fact, he may have had a personality disorder. I don't think they had the best childhood, and that's why Thorn Sr. seemed to

117

run from anything good in his life. Relationship-wise, anyway. But it's also why he was so dedicated to Thorn Jr. and his sister. He was a complicated man. Thorn Jr.'s biological father, on the other hand, wasn't complicated. He did what he wanted and he didn't care who he hurt."

"You think he was a psychopath?" I asked.

"Or a sociopath. Maybe a malignant narcissist," Mom said.

"Wow," I responded. "So you think it's possible Thorn, my Thorn, inherited that?"

"We don't know, honey," my Dad said quickly.

"He's our friend," Mom said quickly. "Thorn is a charming young man, but..."

"But that can be a problem too," I said. "I've seen enough shows about personality disorders."

"We're not saying you shouldn't date him," Dad added. "We're just saying do it with your eyes open. We've been debating telling you about this for a while now, but Thorn's and your relationship didn't seem to be getting much more serious. So, we sat on it."

"You guys remember that the other man in this little triangle I find myself in is a vampire biker who runs an outlaw motorcycle club, right?" I asked.

"People make mistakes," Mom said. "We're not going to tell you what to do. Just know that we support you no matter what, and we're here for you."

"Thanks," I said, and it got quiet again.

A few minutes later, the coroner arrived. He did his thing, cleared the scene, and Thorn left without saying another word to me. He didn't even look in my direction. It was one of his deputies, dressed in jeans and a t-shirt because it was technically his night off, that came over and told me that as soon as the body was removed, I could go home.

"Call us if you need us," my dad said as they rolled away.

I went inside through the back door so I didn't have to go on the porch. Meri had eaten the bacon I'd gotten him while we were in my parents' car. I threw the container away and went into the living room.

Are you okay? The text came through a few minutes after I'd plopped down on the sofa with a book and a bottle of Coke from the fridge. At first, I'd thought that maybe Thorn had a change of heart, but it was from Reggie.

I'm doing okay. I responded.

I would have come over, but your house was like, a crime scene, right? I wasn't sure if I could. I'm sorry. she texted.

It's okay. Thanks for thinking of me. I'm back in the house now.

Do you want me to come over now? she asked.

I think I might go to sleep. We can talk about it tomorrow at the shop. I responded.

So that's still happening?

Of course it is. If you still want the job.

I'll see you then, boss. Call me if you need me. No matter how late. :-) Reggie said.

Night.

A little while later, I had basically the same text exchange with Viv. Except the part about the job, and I told her I'd come in for coffee in the morning.

I must have been exhausted because I fell asleep with my head on the arm of the sofa. My phone was right next to my head, so it woke me up when I got another text a couple of hours later.

Again, it wasn't Thorn. Obviously, he was really mad, and he'd abandoned me because of it. I guess I didn't blame him.

The text was from Azriel. *Are we still on for tonight?*

Well, the woman whose shop I planned to break into was dead. I was probably a suspect. If I was caught breaking into her business, I'd look even more suspicious.

Yeah, we're still totally on. I texted back.

I'll see you in a half hour then. Meet me in the alley behind the store.

See you there.

I was supposed to be there in half an hour, and I needed to walk so no one saw my car. If I hadn't fallen asleep, I'd have been ready to go. As it was, I needed to run upstairs to my room and throw on a black t-shirt and leggings. I tied my hair up into a bun on my head. I didn't have time to do anything with my makeup the old-fashioned way, so I waved my hand over my face and came out with flawless foundation and a perfect smokey eye. It was breaking my rule about not using magic when I didn't absolutely need it, but looking better made me feel better. More confident. I did need that.

"You want me to carry you?" I asked Meri on the way out the door. "I'm not taking a bag. We're traveling light tonight."

"I can keep up," he said.

I locked the front door and rushed down the steps so I could be on that porch as little as possible. At some point, I'd need to do a cleansing ritual to clear the space of the negative energy left by Astra and whoever killed her.

It was quiet, and the moon was new, so Meri and I slipped across my front yard without being seen. We darted across the road, and I climbed over the fence that led into the ancient cemetery located across the street from Hangman's House. The very cemetery that my parents fell in love restoring.

I could hear frogs singing in the nearby creek. Crickets also began their carrying on as we moved among the ancient headstones. The cemetery didn't scare me at all. None of them did, really. But that particular one, I'd played in since I was a child.

That's why the voice that rang out behind me only made me jump half out of my skin. "Hey!"

At first, I thought it was Meri, but he was actually running a little ahead of me. At the sound of the voice, he stopped and whirled around. I did the same, and we came face to face with Brody's ghost.

"You shouldn't be here," I spit. "You're not supposed to be able to come inside the town limits."

"Now, now, Kinsley. You saw me at the diner months ago. You know I can come here anytime I like."

"Technically, you were still outside the town limits. You shouldn't be here now. Not in this place," I said. "Maybe you're not really Brody."

"It's me," he said with a shrug and drifted closer. "I had a little help getting in, if you really must know."

"I bet I know who did that," I said. "But she's dead."

"So?" He almost sounded like a petulant child, but he also drifted closer to me again. I could feel the hatred and malice rolling off of him like an oily, choking smoke.

"You should go," I said. "Go now, or I'm going to dispatch you."

"I'm not afraid of you," he said.

But at that same moment, gray, ghostly hands came up from the grave he was standing on. Abigail Skeenbauer-Trenton, or whatever ghost was just hanging out inside of her plot in the cemetery, reached up and seized Brody's specter. He must not have expected that because he let out a childish shriek. Seconds later, the hands dragged him down into the damp earth.

"Let's keep moving," I said to Meri.

"You don't have to tell me twice."

The rest of the walk to the alley behind what had been Astra's shop was uneventful. When we got there, I almost thought I'd arrived before Azriel until he stepped out from a shadow.

"That's a neat trick," I whispered.

"I'm sure you could manage something similar," he said softly before raising one finger to his lips.

I nodded and opened the back door into Astra's shop. It had been locked, but a little magic was all it took to get through the deadbolt. It took a lot more to get through the warding spells intended to keep other witches out, but she wasn't powerful enough to stop me entirely. It would have been difficult to actually break a dead witch's spell, so I just had to grimace and walk through.

"You okay?" Azriel asked once we were inside and the door was closed.

"Yeah. The door was warded against witches. Let's just say it stung a little to walk through. I'll live."

We were in the back room of the store. It looked a great deal like mine. There was a big open room with shelving, an office off to one side, and a small bathroom off to the other. In fact, it looked almost just like mine.

Especially since my swag bags and decorations were lined up on one of the shelves. "Now I wish I'd brought my car," I said.

"Why is that?" Azriel asked.

"Because my bags and decorations are here," I said and pointed to the shelves.

"Let me call a couple of my guys. They can bring a truck and make quick work of this," Azriel said.

"That's going to be rather conspicuous," I said. "I thought we were going for stealth."

"We'll make quick work of it," he said. "Unless you have another idea? Are you okay with leaving this stuff here and letting the law sort it out?"

"No. Call them," I said. "If your guys can move in the shadows the way you did, the only part to worry about is the truck. Meri and I can camouflage that with magic."

"They will be here in ten minutes," he said after hanging up the phone.

"I'm going to take a look around," I responded. "I want to see if there is anything that might point to why she's dead here."

"You should probably stay away from the front windows."

"I'm going to look in her office," I said. "Meri, why don't you go have a look behind the register."

"What should I do?" Azriel asked.

"Are you taking orders from me now?" I cocked one eyebrow up in disbelief.

"I'd consider it an honor," he said with a smile I couldn't quite read. "But don't let it go to your head."

"We can take a deep dive into the meaning of that when we're done with our little B&E here," I said. "For now, why don't you see if there's anything in these boxes besides extra stock."

"Your wish is my command," he said with an exaggerated bow.

I just rolled my eyes and headed into the office. Once inside, I closed the door so I could turn on the light.

The first thing I found when I sat down at her desk was a notebook with a picture of a cat in a space suit on the front. The notebook was purple, and the cat design was embossed with rainbow metallic.

Inside was just a bunch of creepy drawings and poems written about the beauty of death. It would have been disturbing except that it reminded me of something a teenager would write to try and be edgy.

I closed it and moved it off to the side. Underneath that was a handwritten letter. I looked at the bottom and it was signed by Jemma Crane. The name sounded vaguely familiar, so I read the entire letter.

Apparently, Jemma believe that Astra had stolen her favorite garden gnome. She couldn't get Thorn to do anything about it because there wasn't any proof, so the letter went from begging Astra to give it back to threatening to beat the snot out of her.

"I sympathize, Jemm. I really do," I said and put the letter down.

Astra had a laptop sitting open on the desk. I hit the spacebar and the login screen came up.

I didn't have time to try to go through it, though, because Azriel called out to me. "They're here. Let's go."

"Coming," I said.

Before I left the office, I closed the laptop and unplugged it, taking it with me. I grabbed the letter too. I didn't think that a lawn gnome was a reason to commit murder, but Jemma's letter was pretty unhinged by the end.

Azriel's men loaded the boxes with my bags quickly and took off.

"Do they know where I live?" I asked.

"I'm taking the stuff back to the warehouse," he said. "I don't want you to get caught with it at your house."

"They're going to figure out I got it back eventually," I said. "The whole point is that I have to have it out at the Midnight Magic Festival."

"Let's give it a couple of days to blow over, and then you can *find* it," he said.

"You're the criminal mastermind," I said with a shrug.

129

"What do you have there?" he asked and pointed to the laptop.

"I'd like to figure out who killed her," I said. "I didn't have time to go through the laptop, so I'm taking it with me."

"Now who's the criminal mastermind?" He said. "You realize that's actually stealing, right? It's not the same as taking your stuff back."

"Are you judging me?" I asked.

"Not at all," he said with a smile. "That's a nice laptop too. I can sell it for you when you're done. You could make a few hundred bucks."

"I was thinking of putting it back when I'm done," I said. "But we'll see."

"What are you going to do now?" Azriel asked as we left.

He started to walk down the alley in the opposite direction of my house. I kept walking with him, not really making a decision but just drifting in his wake.

"Would you like to come over?" Azriel asked.

"Or you could come over to my place," I suggested.

"The famous Hangman's House. Maybe I will," he said and took my hand. "I'm sorry."

He started to let go, but I gripped his fingers. "It's all right," I said.

"Do you want to talk about it?"

"On the way," I said. "I assume since you're coming over that you can give me a ride? I walked."

"Oh, now you might just be pushing things," he said.

I stopped in my tracks and just stood there for a moment. After staring at him for a moment with my mouth hanging open, Azriel began to laugh.

"Of course I'll take you home," he said. "My car is right over here."

On the way back to my house, I told Azriel everything about finding Astra's body and then Thorn's subsequent reaction. I didn't share with him the things my mother and father had told me because I hadn't processed it.

"Do you want me to pull my car into the garage?" Azriel asked. "It he comes by, he'll see my car here."

"That's sweet of you to offer," I said. "But no. If you're in my life, I'm not going to hide it. I won't hide you."

Chapter Five

Once we were inside, I wasn't sure what to do. I didn't have any video games, and we'd already watched a movie.

"You want me to take a crack at that laptop?" Azriel asked as we sat there awkwardly.

Technically, I could use magic to get into it, but I kinda wanted to see what he had in mind. "Sure. What are you going to do? Are you some sort of super hacker or something?"

"I wouldn't say that," Azriel said as I handed him the laptop. "But it wouldn't take a super hacker to get into someone's laptop anyway."

He sat down on my sofa and opened the laptop up on my coffee table. I joined him, but not too close. Meri, on the other hand, jumped up on the coffee table and practically sat down on Azriel's right hand.

Azriel didn't seem to mind. He cracked his knuckles and let his fingers fly over the keyboard. "There you go," he said after a minute.

I reached out and turned the laptop toward me. Sure enough, he was in.

"It's just a work laptop," I said after looking at the sparse icons on the desktop. "There's nothing personal here."

"Could she have used magic to conceal it?" he offered.

"I can check." I closed my eyes and hovered my hands over the keyboard. "There's no magic at work on the computer at all. I think it's just a business laptop."

"I can go," Azriel said. "It's getting late."

"Or we can watch another movie. There's also that documentary series that everyone is watching on Netflix," I offered.

"The one with the snake guy?" Azriel asked.

"Yeah, that one. It's cheesy, I know. But everyone is talking about it."

"Sure," Azriel said. "I don't have anything better to do."

"Wow."

He laughed. "You should take it as a compliment that I don't have anything better to do than watch documentaries with you."

I put the show on auto-play on my television, and the next thing I knew, it was morning. I'd

134

fallen asleep on the sofa. Passed out would be more appropriate.

Azriel was gone. He'd covered me up with a blanket, and I'd curled up into a ball. Meri was snoozing at my feet.

Out of nowhere, I felt a stabbing pain in my chest. It sucked the wind out of me. I grabbed my phone and checked for a message from Thorn. The idea of losing him was suddenly and overwhelmingly painful. He hadn't just been my boyfriend. He was my best friend. I didn't know what the universe was trying to tell me about Azriel, but I couldn't just throw Thorn away.

Before I could really think about what I was doing, I called him.

"What is it?" he asked gruffly when he answered, but he answered. I shouldn't have read too far into that. He was the sheriff after all, but I still clung to it like a little seed of hope.

"I'm sorry," I said. "I've been stupid. I should have trusted you. I should have trusted that I could talk to you."

"I don't think that I have time for this, Kinsley." Thorn let out a sigh. "You realize that you're a suspect in Astra Argent's murder, right? You're the suspect. The only suspect right now."

"Are you going to arrest me?"

"You know that I'm not."

"I don't want you getting in trouble for me," I said.

"Kinsley, I would lose my job and get run out of this town before I ever did anything to hurt you," Thorn said. "I know you didn't kill Astra, so I'm not going to arrest you."

"Why did you tell me that you were going to break things off with me if you'd decided not to do it? Didn't you know how much that would upset me?" I had to know why he'd done it.

"Because it was the truth. Because I was hurting," Thorn said. "Another man kissed you, and you didn't exactly make it sound like you were upset about it. That and whatever this connection you have with him. I don't know what that's about, but I know it hurts. I screwed up, Kinsley. I should have protected you from that hurt, and I didn't. I'm sorry."

I did not expect him to admit he was wrong and apologize. I suddenly wished that I'd just waited and talked to him about the whole thing. I wished I'd been a gawd-dang adult for a couple of hours instead of running to the first port in a storm.

"I broke into Astra's shop last night. Azriel helped me. The good news is that I found my swag bags and decorations. The bad news is that I let Azriel take them back to his clubhouse to protect them for me... and I really don't want you to dump me. I think that I've been foolish, and I don't understand why. But that doesn't matter because I have been."

"Did anything happen between you two?"

"I let him break into Astra's laptop. Which I also stole. I was going to put it back."

"Is that all?"

"He stayed at the house for a while last night. I invited him to watch that new docu series on the snake guy. I fell asleep, though. He was gone this morning when I woke up."

"I thought we were going to watch that." Thorn sounded genuinely hurt.

"I found a dead woman on my porch last night, and you left without speaking to me. I thought it was over," I said. "But I didn't see any of the show. I crashed. So, if you don't hate me, we can still watch it."

He was silent for a while. "If you're breaking into places and doing necromancy with him, then Kinsley, why are you calling me?"

"Because I woke up this morning and everything felt wrong. It was kind of like being hit with lightning or inspiration. I don't know. Something like that. I felt very clearly that what I wanted was you, and you hadn't texted me. Even to see if I was okay. So, I called."

"I'm sorry. I should have at least checked in on you. I let my anger and jealousy get in the way. I'm better than that, and I need to be better than that for you."

"Are you going to arrest me for breaking into Astra's shop?"

"And have to face off with your mother and Amelda? No thanks," he said with a chuckle.

That sound unclenched something in my chest. I let out a breath I didn't know I was holding.

"What do we do, Thorn? Where do we go from here?"

"I've got to get started on finding out who killed Astra," Thorn said. "I'll come by later and see you. You're going into the shop today?"

"I am. Reggie is going to start working with me today. I hired her to assist me in the shop."

"I need to hire a new deputy," Thorn said. "I've got two interviews this afternoon. Hopefully, one of them will work out. I need to stop working doubles almost every day."

"Well, have a good day. I can't wait to see you later," I said.

"You too, baby. I love you, Kinsley."

"I love you too," I said without even having to think about it.

After we hung up, I rushed upstairs to take a shower. While I was getting ready, I noticed that my hair was turning lighter again. My eyes were emerald green as well. A much darker shade than normal but not purple. They weren't black. While my hair and eyes were darker, I looked significantly more like myself.

As I left the house for work, I noticed a calm had come over me as well. There had been a darkness skittering around under my skin for the last couple of days. It was like static, and I didn't really notice it until it was gone.

Something had a hold on me, and it had let go. At the time, I didn't put two and two together because I was just so relieved.

I drove to my shop with the radio on and my window down. It didn't bother me when people stared because I was belting out a power ballad at the top of my lungs. Some people scowled while others smiled and waved.

After I parked my car in front of my shop, I hurried across the square to grab a coffee from Viv's. She had a line, so while I waited, I shot off a text to Reggie to ask her what she wanted.

Caramel macchiato with extra caramel. she texted back. *Lots of extra caramel.*

It will be waiting for you when you arrive. I answered.

I'm just about to head out the door.

"You look so much better," Viv said when I stepped up to the counter. "Your usual?"

"That and a large Caramel macchiato with lots of extra caramel. Reggie is going to start working with me today," I said.

"Oh, that's great news. I'm a little jealous of you two getting to work together. I'll be stuck over here," Viv said as she started to make the drinks.

"We'll come see you often. I promise."

I was unlocking the door to the shop when Reggie arrived. I handed her the Caramel macchiato and we went inside.

Even with the lights on, it was pretty dim inside. The plastic sheeting kept the majority of the light out, but it was better than it all being wide open.

I was turning on my computer and getting ready for my day when it all got ripped down. Dennis was standing on the other side smiling. Then he saw my coffee and his face fell.

"Dang it. I should have grabbed a coffee before I got started. I knew I was forgetting something."

"I'll run and grab you one," Reggie offered. "Unless you've got something you need me to do right now?"

"No, go ahead," I said. "I'm not going to open until Dennis is done anyway. I don't want customers tripping over him and getting in his way."

"Thank you kindly," Dennis said. "This is probably going to take me a few hours."

"Right. I guess I wasn't thinking about that," I said. "Well, if we decide to go do something else, is it all right to leave you here?"

"I can manage. I won't steal anything."

"I didn't think you would," I said. "There's a bathroom in the back but... the commode is kind of tricky. You might want to just use the one over at the Brew Station. Plus, you can grab more coffee."

I was waiting outside for Reggie when she got back with Dennis's coffee. I felt like I needed to stay busy, and since I couldn't work, I thought I'd stick my nose into Astra's death.

"Everything okay?" Reggie asked.

"Yeah, it's going to be a few hours before the windows are done. Do you want to get involved in some shenanigans?"

"What did you have in mind?"

"Okay, so I broke into Astra's shop last night..."

"You didn't!" Reggie said with a huge smile.

"I did, and I found a letter to her from her neighbor accusing her of stealing her favorite garden gnome."

"You think she was killed over a garden gnome?" Reggie asked.

"The letter was from a woman named Jemma Crane. It became rather... unhinged at the end."

"Oh, yeah. That lady is nuts. She's completely off her rocker."

"So you think it's possible she killed Astra over the stolen gnome?" I asked.

"I think if it's possible that anyone would kill someone over a garden gnome, it would be Jemma."

"Does that mean you're in?" I asked as I finally started the car.

"I even know where we're going. I'll give you directions," Reggie said.

I backed my car out of the parking spot, and we were on our way.

It was immediately obvious which house was Jemma's. Not only was it painted bright pink with lime green shutters, but there were garden gnomes and little statues everywhere. They were lined up along the porch railing and down both sides of the sidewalk.

In the middle of each side of the yard was a large purple dragon surrounded by white flowers. At the feet of the dragons were even more little gnomes that were in dancing poses. Some of them had their tiny fingers stretched up to the sky, while others appeared to be doing the twist.

I didn't know which side Astra lived on, but an older woman came out of the house on the left and sat down her porch. That meant Astra's house was on the right. Not that it mattered, we were there for Jemma.

At that time, I had no plans on going into Astra's house. Not because it didn't need to be searched. I just hadn't thought of it yet.

Bizarrely enough, it felt like the little gnomes were watching us as we walked up the sidewalk and then the porch steps. I tried to ignore it even though it unnerved me more than I expected. I could easily deal with demons and angry ghosts. I'd used necromancy recently, and I was supposed to be one of the most powerful witches in the world, but something about those little statues creeped me the heck out. There was a very good reason for that, but I wouldn't figure it out until it was too late.

I was reaching for Reggie's arm to stop her so I could tell her something wasn't right, but she'd already knocked by the time I said her name. "Reggie."

"What is it?" she asked as she stepped back from the threshold.

"This place is just weird," I said and looked around. "Don't all these little gnomes make you feel weird?"

She chuckled. "I never imagined you'd have a garden gnome phobia."

"I'm not really afraid of garden gnomes. It's *these* garden gnomes," I said.

"I think it's a little weird that there are so many of them, but I'm not getting a horror movie vibe off this place, if that's what you're asking," she said. "And if I am missing something creepy, then all the better that we're here. If she is a weirdo psycho killer with a garden gnome fetish, we'll figure it out."

"What if she tries to kill us?" I asked. I had my magic so technically, there was no reason to be afraid. Still, I didn't want to whip it out and use it in front of Reggie for this...

"I'll shoot her," Reggie said matter-of-factly. "I've got a gun in my purse."

"What?"

"I have my concealed carry permit," she said. "I finally qualified, so I've been going to the range and practicing. I'm packing heat."

"You never told me about that," I said.

Reggie shrugged. "Now you know. So, don't worry. I'll protect us if it turns out Jemma is bat-snot insane and tries to axe us to death or something."

"You're entirely too casual about this," I said, but I had to smile.

The door opened before Reggie could say anything else, and I got my first look at Jemma Crane. She wore a hot pink dress that reminded me of something a 1950's housewife would wear except the pattern on it was... something I won't repeat. Let's just say that at first, I thought it was some sort of fish or perhaps a reptile. But, nope. It was the outline of male

146

anatomy. There, I said it. I almost choked when I realized what it was. The dress had to have been something she made for herself. Even Reggie's jaw hung open for a split second too long.

"How can I help you ladies?" Jemma asked brightly.

Her bleached blonde hair was pulled up into a high ponytail, and little troll earrings with rainbow hair hung from her ears. She also wore rainbow eyeshadow with bright red lipstick. Her wrists were heavy with colorful enamel bracelets in pink, green, and white.

"I wanted to talk to you about your neighbor Astra Argent," I said.

"Oh, yeah, that chick is dead," Jemma said with a big smile. "Normally, I wouldn't get so excited about someone dying, but she was just awful. Do you want to come in? I lived next door to her, so I probably know more than anyone else about her in this town."

"Sure," Reggie said. "We'd love to."

When I shot Reggie a look, she just patted her purse and then shot gun fingers at me. "Thank you," I said to Jemma.

The inside of the house was as colorfully decorated at the outside of the house. It even rivaled Jemma. Fortunately, there weren't any totems to male anatomy. I'd halfway expected that. But there were more garden gnomes. Or just gnomes in general. I wasn't sure that they were garden gnomes when they lived inside the house.

Jemma led us into a parlor furnished with white wicker furniture. Reggie and I sat down on the hot pink cushions adorning the wicker sofa.

"I'm going to get us some tea," Jemma said. "Or would you prefer lemonade?" Her voice lilted in a way that indicated she hoped we wanted the lemonade.

"I'd like some lemonade," I said.

"Oh, me too," Reggie agreed.

"Good," Jemma said in sing-song voice. "I'll be right back then."

"This place is weird," Reggie admitted when Jemma was gone. "I didn't feel it until we were inside."

"Do you want to leave? I dragged you into this. We can bolt while she's getting the lemonade," I said.

"No. It's okay. I just wanted you to know that I'm feeling it too. I guess it just took me longer to pick up on it."

"All right," I said. "We'll try to make it quick."

"No, we're here. We might as well get what we came for."

A moment later, Jemma reappeared with the lemonade.

The pitcher and both glasses were covered with yellow and white daisies. She carried them into the room on a bright pink wood tray and set it down on the glass and wicker table right in front of us.

"Thank you," I said as Jemma handed me a cool glass.

"So, what did you want to know about Astra?" Jemma asked as she handed Reggie a glass. She then sat down in the chair to our right and smoothed her... interesting dress over her knees. "There's so much material there, I'll let you tell me where we're starting."

"I actually have something specific I want to ask you about. It has to do with you," I said.

"Oh, the gnome she stole." Jemma's eyes narrowed and her entire expression darkened.

"How did you know about that? Was she bragging about it? I bet she was bragging about it."

And just like that, Jemma was near hysterics. It did look highly suspicious that she was getting so bent out of shape so fast. I could see her going nuts and killing someone. Thankfully, at the time, she wasn't angry with us.

Or, so I thought.

"She left a letter from you sitting out in her shop, and I happened to see it," I said and was amazed at how fast the lie dripped off my tongue. I reasoned with myself that the police lied to suspects all the time. It wasn't that my character was being eaten away by the darkness.

"Were you hanging around in her shop or something?" Jemma's answering of my question with a question did not escape my notice. "I thought you didn't like her. Maybe I misunderstood."

"No, you didn't. I've had to go into her shop a couple of times to confront her about things she's done. I saw it one of those times."

Jemma visibly relaxed. "Oh, I see. Okay. Well, yes. I did have to write her a letter. I hope you won't think less of me because I had to write a letter instead of confronting her face to face the way you did."

"Not at all. You're quite an excellent writer." I hoped that flattery would get her talking.

"Thank you," she said with a huge grin. "How's the lemonade?"

"It's delicious," I said and took another sip.

"Yeah, it's great," Reggie said before stretching her arms above her head and yawning. "Oof. Sorry about that. I guess I didn't sleep well last night."

"Have another glass," Jemma said and refilled Reggie's glass before she could say anything. "The sugar will perk you right up."

"Thanks," Reggie said before downing half the glass.

"Are you sure you're enjoying it?" Jemma asked me. "I can get you some tea instead."

"It's very good," I said. "Some of the best lemonade I've ever had. I'm just not as thirsty as my friend."

When I took another drink, Jemma seemed pleased. Why her preoccupation with us downing the lemonade didn't strike me as odd, given what we knew about how crazy she was, it should have been a red flag. At the time, I just took it as her being weird. Which given our surroundings and our host, wasn't weird anymore.

"So, yes, I wrote her the letter," Jemma continued. "I went out to my garden one morning, and my favorite gnome was missing. The little dickens can't just get up and walk off on their own."

Jemma let out a weird laugh. It sounded like it bordered on the verge of madness, but there was something else as well. It was almost as if she knew she'd let something slip. She was watching us too. Perhaps wanting to know if we'd caught it. I'd caught that there was something, but I wasn't sure what?

Was she hiding that the gnomes could move on their own? But, that couldn't be right. That would mean that...

Before the idea could fully form in my mind, Reggie slumped back in her chair. I looked over at her to see what she was up to, and she started to snore. I began to feel a little tired too, so I quickly sat the glass of lemonade down.

I healed myself from the effects of whatever she'd put in the lemonade as Meri jumped up on the coffee table and put himself between me and Jemma. "You drugged us," I said.

"Why isn't it working on her?" Jemma demanded, but she wasn't talking to me.

I looked to the side and saw that she was talking to a row of garden gnomes lined up on a side table against the wall. While I expected that at any moment, they might come to life and pull little knives from behind their backs, they just stood there staring at her. I shook my head as if to clear it of the dumb idea that the gnomes might actually come to life.

Jemma reached for Meri, but he swatted her hand away with his tiny paw. It probably wouldn't have worked except that he scratched her good.

"Leave my cat alone," I said. "You try to touch him again, and you're going to find out my claws are far worse than his."

"Why didn't it work on you? It should have worked on you. You're like her... aren't you?"

"I'm going to need you to sit down and shut up," I said. "I'm calling the sheriff."

Meri hissed at Jemma, and she plopped down into the chair. She kept babbling about how her lemonade didn't work on me while I called Thorn.

"What are you doing?" he asked after I told him where I was.

"I saw a letter from this Jemma Crane lady to Astra. I wanted to ask her about it. Anyway, she drugged Reggie and she tried to drug me. She's nuts."

"I'll be right there," he said. "Are you okay? Are you safe?"

"Of course. Reggie's got a gun in her purse. I'm going to wake her up now," I said.

"She's got a gun?" Thorn asked. "No, wait. You can tell me later. I'm getting in my cruiser now. I'll be right there."

As soon as he hung up, I put my phone in my pocket and used my magic to bring Reggie out of her stupor. "What! What's going on?" Reggie asked as she sprang up off of the sofa.

"This crazy... lady drugged you. You need to get your gun out of your purse and hold it on her," I said.

"Wait, but how did you not pass out? How did you wake me?" Reggie asked as she rubbed her eyes with her fists.

"We'll talk about that later. Thorn's on his way here, and I figured you could put that gun to good use. You said you knew how to use it, right?"

"I do," Reggie said proudly.

She got the gun out of her purse holster and held it on Jemma. I started to wander around the room and look at the garden gnomes. I could swear they were looking at me. It was an odd feeling, but their eyes weren't moving.

"I'm going to go in the kitchen and see if I can figure out what she drugged us with," I said. "Are you okay?"

"I'm good," Reggie said. "If she tries anything nutty, I'll shoot her."

"Did you hear that, Jemma? She's going to shoot you if you don't sit there and behave."

Jemma just kept babbling about the lemonade not working. I offered Reggie a shrug, and she motioned for me to go.

The kitchen was about what you'd expect. Gnomes stood at attention lined along the counters with their backs pushed against the backsplash. There were a couple on top of the refrigerator and three more sitting near the back door.

On the counter near the sink sat a small bottle with a cork stopper. Inside were dried purple leaves. I pulled the cork out and sniffed the leaves. I couldn't identify the smell, but it definitely wasn't regular flower petals. Since I didn't have time to identify the contents before Thorn arrived, I stashed the bottle in my purse. I'd figure it out later.

I heard a car pull up in the driveway and looked out the kitchen window. It was Thorn's cruiser, so I went out the back door and signaled for him to follow me in through the back door.

"She's in a sunroom-type parlor," I said. "I'll show you."

I led Thorn into the room, and Reggie put her gun away. Jemma was still there babbling to herself.

"Do you have any evidence she drugged you?" Thorn said.

"Well, I told you she drugged me. So, there's that." I found myself a little annoyed that he even asked.

"I know, and I believe you, but if you want me to arrest her, I need something proving she drugged you," he said.

"You could take the lemonade glasses," Reggie said calmly. "It was in there. I'm also verifying that I indeed passed out after drinking it."

"All right. I'll bag the glasses and get them over to the state police lab," Thorn said.

I also had the little bottle of what I assumed she used, but I had my doubts that they would be able to identify what it was. Something was off about Jemma, but I hadn't put my finger on it yet. I didn't want to hand the entire supply over to Thorn because I wouldn't be able to figure it out myself. Plus, I didn't have proof that it was what she used. I'd just found it in the kitchen. The lab could analyze the glasses using their methods, and I'd use my methods.

"Ma'am, can you tell me what happened here?" Thorn asked.

Jemma turned her head toward him, but she looked past him. Again, it seemed she was looking at the gnomes behind her.

"It didn't work on them," she said. "Well, it worked on that one." Jemma pointed at Reggie, but then she turned to me. "But it didn't work on her. That one is weird. She's not right. It should have worked. This is the second time it hasn't worked. Would you like some lemonade, Sheriff?"

When Jemma asked the last part, the cloudy confusion left her eyes. She plastered a huge smile on her face. Suddenly she was back from wherever she'd gone.

"No, thank you. Can you tell me what happened here today? These ladies say you drugged them. I need you to tell me about that."

"That's crazy. We were just having a chat about my ex-neighbor," she said. "How did you get in here?"

Thorn turned back to me. "I'm going to call an ambulance. I think it would be better if I had her taken in on a psych hold for right now."

"The hospital!" Jemma said and practically leapt out of her chair. "I don't want to go to the hospital again! NO! NO! NO! I can't leave my babies!"

Thorn ended up having to put her in cuffs while we waited for the ambulance. He took her out to his squad car to wait, and I looked around. Thorn wanted us to leave the house with him, but on the off chance that by "my babies" she meant pets, he let us look around.

As I expected, there were no pets. She must have been talking about the garden gnomes. I took one last look out the back door before we left. When I'd gone out there to let Thorn in, I noticed something that caught my attention.

In the center of the yard was a stone pillar with a rectangular top. It was almost like an altar, and it was empty. It had to be the place where her favorite gnome sat until it disappeared. There were circular rows of purple flowers around it and in between those were more gnomes. They were set up to look like they were dancing around or worshiping whatever was on the altar. The purple flowers were most likely what was in the bottle in my purse. They didn't look like any flowers I'd ever seen before. I almost picked one, but thought better of going near them. Instead, I took a few photos.

The ambulance finally arrived, and Jemma went wild. The paramedics had to sedate her and then strap her down. I watched them give her three shots of whatever it was when the first one had no effect and the second barely stopped her thrashing, kicking, and biting.

She scratched Thorn across the face, and I had to heal him once the ambulance was gone and Reggie was in the car scrolling through her phone. The wound was weird too. It smelled almost floral, and Thorn said it burned worse than any other scratch he'd ever gotten. "It's like acid."

There wasn't any time to discuss it further as Thorn had to follow the ambulance to the hospital. He said he'd had it happen too many times where the paramedics didn't agree with his assessment, so the hospital let the patient go. He wanted to make sure Jemma was held for the full seventy-two hours. The only way to know for sure was to sit in the ER with her and make the doctor see his point of view.

I walked back over to the car and let Meri in. After I slid behind the steering wheel, Reggie put her phone down in her lap. "The cat can talk, right?" she asked.

I wasn't sure what to say, so I just looked at her.

"Don't lie to me, Kinsley. Please don't lie anymore. I'm starting to feel like I'm going insane when I'm around you, and I don't like that. Something is different about you and that cat. I know it."

I didn't want to lie to her anymore, and it made me uncomfortable that she felt like I was gaslighting her. I'd never intended to make Reggie feel crazy, but it didn't help that the magic veil that protected humans from feeling this way around us didn't seem as effective on her.

"You think the cat can talk," I said. "What else?"

She narrowed her eyes at me and seemed to be searching my face for clues about what I was getting at. "I know I've seen ghosts. It's not pareidolia or whatever nonsense fake psychological thing they make up to explain it away. They're real. I've seen them. There's a creepy one that hangs out in the back of the shop. That, and I've seen people around Coventry do things. I don't know how to explain it, though. I've seen them do unexplainable things, but everyone else ignores it. Am I nuts? I'd have accepted that I had some sort of mental illness, but it doesn't happen anywhere else. At least, I've never been or lived somewhere else that it happened... And all these tourists and ghost hunters flock to Coventry like they're drawn to whatever it is, but then it's all in good fun. They find what they're looking for, and then explain it away themselves. It's insane. Do you know how many YouTube videos I've watched where people in Coventry have actually caught paranormal activity on camera, but they don't believe it. Even the people in the comments make jokes or just say it's fake. But it's not!"

"You're right," I said.

"I'm right?" Her eyes widened. Reggie hadn't expected me to just agree. "All of it?"

"All of it," I said.

"Yeah, she's telling you the truth," Meri piped up from the back seat. "Now you're in on it."

"Holy crap. He can talk," she said. "So, what does that make you?"

"I'm a witch," I said with a shrug.

"Holy crap," Reggie said. "Back in school... Those girls who were bullying you... They said you used some sort of power on them, but nobody believe them. You really did. That's why you got pulled out of school?"

"Yeah," I said. "I was only allowed to go to regular school as long as I didn't do anything like that, and then I did."

"They had it coming," Reggie said.

"They did, but I knew better. I lost my temper."

"So the stuff that you sell in the shop, it's really magical?" Reggie asked.

"It is and it isn't. Magic is all around us, Reggie. Whether something is magical or not is really in the hands of the person using it."

"Why are you telling me this?" she asked. "Why don't more people know?"

"I'm telling you because you're my best friend, and I can't let you go on feeling crazy around me. It's not right. I was going to tell you eventually anyway, but I had to heal you from whatever Jemma gave you. I figured I wasn't going to be able to put it off any longer."

"I just don't understand how this hasn't gotten out."

"Because there's a magical veil over Coventry that makes regular people ignore paranormal things they see, but there are people like you who it doesn't work as well on. That's one of the reasons ghost hunters flock to Coventry. It's why it has a witchy reputation. Over time, there have been enough like you that the word has sort of gotten out. It's just that when people get there, they have a good time and nothing else. The magic keeps them from seeing anything that could be concrete evidence."

"But you moved away from Coventry? Why?"

"That's a long story about me not wanting to be a witch. I'll tell you on the way. We'd better go back and see if Dennis is done with the windows."

Chapter Six

The temporary windows were done when we got back, and Dennis was sitting in his truck drinking coffee and eating a croissant sandwich from the Brew Station. There was also a woman standing at the door waiting for us.

I walked over to Dennis first. "Do you know who she is? Did she say anything to you?" I asked after he rolled his truck window down.

"No. I figured you knew her. She's been standing there for a while."

"I don't recognize her at all," I said. "That's okay. I'll talk to her. Do you need anything else from me?"

"No, ma'am. I'm just finishing up my lunch. I'll let Castor know when I'll be back with the permanent windows, okay?"

"Sounds good," I said and left him to finish his food.

"Can I help you?" I asked the woman standing by my shop's door.

She was dressed in all black, but the dress looked Victorian, as did the little pointed leather boots on her feet. She looked at me over the top of her tiny round spectacles, and I could tell right away that she was a witch. Not a Skeenbauer or Tuttlesmith, though, and not from Coventry.

"My name is Fortuna Barclay," she said and sniffed the air as if she smelled something foul. "I'm related to Astra Argent. I'm here to handle her burial arrangements, and I was told that you were who I should talk to about her death."

"Who told you that?" I asked. I wanted to make a mental note of who to be wary of and also to possibly turn into a goat.

"The funeral director who took possession of her body after the coroner released it said that you were the one who killed her. He also said that you were a rival businessperson."

"Why don't we step inside?" I said.

She didn't seem particularly friendly, and I was concerned that her statements would draw attention. If Fortuna was going to accuse me of murder, she could do it inside where no one would hear her. At least until I had some customers come in. I left the closed sign up and locked the door behind us to ensure that didn't happen, though.

"I'd go in the back and give you two some privacy," Reggie said, "but I'm not doing that. I'll be over there dusting shelves."

She grabbed the duster from behind the counter and started dusting shelves as far away from the front counter as she could get without actually going into the back. Meri followed behind her, but he stayed where he could see me.

"I'm sorry..." I started to say.

"Don't say you're sorry about my loss when we both know you're not," Fortuna interrupted. "Honestly, I didn't know Astra that well anymore, so I can't say it's even that much of a loss."

That struck me as odd, but I just said, "Okay then, what can I do for you?"

"Well, the reason I came to Coventry instead of one of the other family members is that Astra owed me money. She owed me a lot of money, actually, and prior to her death, I had no reason to believe she'd pay me back. Mostly because she sent me an email stating that I shouldn't hold my breath waiting for it," Fortuna said. "It was rather rude, and my mother and husband told me not to loan her the money, but there's a fool born every minute. You know?"

"You didn't know her very well, but you loaned her a large sum of money?" I couldn't help but wonder if that was motive for murder.

"I knew Astra well when she was a child. We were close then. I watched her a great deal for her mother, but Astra grew away from the coven as she got older. I loaned her the money partially because of the sweet girl I once knew and partly because she promised to pay me back plus cut me in on the profits from the shop."

"But she told you that wasn't going to happen? How could she have known that? She hadn't been open for more than couple of days," I said.

"She said that you were determined to drive her out of business and that you'd already gone to rather extreme measures to ruin her," Fortuna said. "She said you broke into her business and set her back for months."

Classic projection. Astra accused me of doing the very thing she'd tried to do to me. "That's reversed," I said. "She broke into my shop. Smashed my windows and stole some very important stock."

Fortuna let out a sigh. "It figures. What did she take? I can go over there and get it back for you."

"It's already been handled," I said.

Fortuna raised one eyebrow. "I won't ask you to elaborate as I'm hoping to establish a mutually beneficial business relationship with you myself."

"Oh?" I asked. "You mean you're not here to size me up? You don't intend to take over Astra's shop?"

"Not hardly," Fortuna said with a laugh that let me know she found the idea ludicrous. "I have a life elsewhere. I'm just here in the hopes of recovering some of the money I loaned her. I was hoping to do that by selling you her stock. The coven decided I could do that, keep what I'm owed, and give the rest to the family. Seeing as how you run a very similar shop, I thought you might have use for the stuff. Our coven could use it, but I'd rather have the money."

"Right. That makes sense," I said. "Well, did you have a price in mind? Or did you need me to price everything for you?"

"I heard all her records were on her business laptop," Fortuna said. "But I left them at the shop, and the laptop has grown legs. I don't suppose you know anything about that."

"Um..."

"Anyway, should it turn up, the value of her stock is there. I'm not looking to make a profit. If I sell everything to you at cost, I should get back what I loaned her. So, keep an eye out for the computer, okay?"

"I will," I said.

"If you should happen across it and find a total for the stock, you can let me know tomorrow if you're willing to pay. Otherwise, I've got to start contacting auctioneers and wholesale companies to get quotes. I think it would be better for both of us if you are interested, though."

"Okay," I said. "I'll see you tomorrow then?"

"Yes. I'm staying at the hotel over by the Italian restaurant. I'll come here tomorrow morning after breakfast and before I leave town."

"Deal," I said.

After that, I let her out of the shop. I was about to turn the sign to open, and Reggie said "Wait!"

"What?" I almost jumped because she'd snuck up behind me.

"We need to get some lunch. I'm starving," she said.

I laughed. "How about I give you some money and you run over to the Brew Station? That way, I can open the shop."

"Are you sure?" Reggie asked.

"Yeah, there looks to be a ghost tour about to wrap up over there in the square. I want to open before they scatter," I said. "Don't tell Viv what I told you. Not yet, please. I'll find a way to tell her soon."

"I'm glad she doesn't know yet," Reggie said.

"What? Why?" I said with a chuckle.

"It means you told me first," Reggie said. "I know it's juvenile, but it makes me feel special. Like, you really mean it when you say I'm your best friend."

"Of course I mean it," I said. "I wouldn't say something like that if I didn't mean it."

"Cool," Reggie replied. "Anyway, what do you want to eat?"

"The turkey, bacon, and Havarti croissant with kettle chips and a large hazelnut latte," I said as I fished the money out of my purse. "This should be enough for that and whatever you want."

"I will be right back," she said happily.

As soon as she was gone, I turned the sign to open and watched her cross the square. The ghost tour was just about over, and some of the tourists were already looking in the store's direction. I assumed they'd all make their way over once the tour was over. They didn't have any choice because Astra's store was closed.

The Midnight Magic Festival was coming up that weekend, and the town would start decorating for it by the end of the week. Someone from the maintenance crew would be by to pick up the decorations I'd made to decorate our side of the square. I'd have to figure out how to get the swag bags and belladonna garland back from Azriel. I'd made wreaths out of other poisonous flowers as well, but Azriel had it all.

While I waited for customers, I went to my shelves and grabbed a quartz crystal, some

172

dried lavender, and a dram of Fiery Wall of Protection oil. Last, I picked up a small purple velvet bag.

I stood behind the counter and put the items in the bag. After closing it and tying the little drawstrings in a knot, I envisioned a snake of white light coming out of the bag and encircling me. The last step was tying the protection mojo to one of the belt loops on my jeans. I'd made it specifically to protect me from psychic vampires, and I'd done it almost unconsciously when I thought of Azriel.

Was that it? Had he tricked me into opening an empathic link with him using his dog as bait? My skin prickled and my blood boiled at the thought.

Before I could get myself too worked up, a handful of chattering women came into the shop from the ghost tour. "Oh, it smells divine in here. What is that?" one of them asked.

"I have a wide assortment of oils and herbs, ladies. Your energy will draw you to the ones that are best for you," I said and they tittered excitedly. "Let me know if you need any assistance."

They were walking around for a long time picking stuff up off the shelves and bringing it up to the counter for me to hold. I thought about getting shopping baskets and made a mental note to check the internet for prices. Reggie returned with the food and we stood up front and ate while the women shopped. A few more people trickled in, and everyone wanted to know where we got the food. I happily told them it was from the Brew Station across the square. Viv was going to get a small rush of afternoon business when the women were done shopping.

Eventually most of them came up together and checked out. They left and I watched them walk in a group over to Viv's to get food.

The same thing happened again when the next ghost tour got over. After they were gone, it was about time to close.

"What are you going to do tonight?" Reggie asked as she was sweeping.

"I have to go home and look up how much Astra's stock is worth so I can give Fortuna a quote in the morning. I do have the stolen laptop after all. What are you going to do?"

"I need to go over to the nursing home and sign some paperwork. I'm going to have dinner with my grandmother too."

"Please don't let me forget tomorrow to find out about your health insurance," I said. "I'm sorry I forgot today."

"Hey, it's been a big day, but I'll definitely remind you tomorrow," she said.

"Do you need a ride to the nursing home?"

"Nope, I've got my car running again."

Reggie had purchased a car that was older than mine a couple of months back. It didn't run more than it ran. She'd get it fixed and something else would break, but it would always be fixed over the weekend. I suspected it was her secret man helping her.

"Now that I've told you my secret, are you going to come clean about your relationship?" I said.

"I wasn't hiding it from you, I swear. I just didn't want to jinx anything. It's been very casual up until recently."

"So casual that he's always fixing your car? That doesn't sound casual." I laughed. "That sounds like a man taking care of his woman."

"I promise I'll tell you all about it soon," she said and blushed.

Chapter Seven

After Reggie and I said our goodbyes, I closed the shop for the day and went home. I still had work to do, but I needed Astra's computer to do it.

Back at home, I got Meri some bacon as a late afternoon snack and made myself some hot cocoa with a half scoop of instant espresso. It was just enough for a pick-me-up, but it wouldn't keep me up at night.

I set Astra's laptop up at the kitchen table and put the bottle of dried purple leaves from Jemma's house on the counter so I wouldn't forget about them. When Meri finished his bacon, he jumped into the chair next to me and curled up for a nap.

Azriel had removed the password protection from Astra's computer when he broke into it for me, so all I had to do was boot it up and find the folder with her receipts. Adding up how much she paid for the stock was easy, and it took me about a half an hour. When I was done, I emailed myself the totals and receipts so I could show Fortuna the next morning.

When I was done, I closed the windows and was about to shut the laptop when I saw something. It was a folder marked "photoes", and I must have ignored it before because I didn't notice the misspelling.

I double-clicked the folder, and inside I found hundreds of pictures of people. They all looked to be random strangers, and I had no idea why she would have pictures of them in her laptop. The other strange thing about the photos was that they all appeared to be from different sources. Some looked like they'd been taken without the subject knowing they were being photographed. It was as if they were being stalked. Others looked to be professional headshots, and still others appeared to possibly be scans from newspaper stories.

On a whim, I emailed the folder's contents to myself too. I didn't know what it all meant, but I planned to return the laptop to Fortuna, and I wanted to have the photos. It was just a hunch.

I got a text from Thorn a few minutes after I finished. *I think I finally found my new hire. I might be able to stop working late soon.*

I take it your interview is going well. I'm so happy. I responded.

I think you're really going to like her. She reminds me a lot of you. If I hire her, I'll have to introduce you. was his text.

Despite the fact that I knew I was being stupid, I felt myself prickle with jealousy. Somewhere in the back of my mind, I felt myself get insecure. If he hired a deputy that was a lot like me, but that hadn't upset him the way I had, would he really need me anymore?

I pushed aside the thoughts that Thorn was hiring my replacement and went into the kitchen. The first thing I grabbed from the refrigerator was an onion. I cried while I was chopping it, and it was entirely possible that they were real tears. Tears from frustration and not sadness. I felt silly for putting myself in a position where jealousy was even a possibility. I knew that if I hadn't put a strain on my relationship with Thorn, I wouldn't be jealous. I wouldn't feel threatened by his excitement over hiring a woman to work closely with him that reminded him of me.

When the onions were done, I threw them into the Dutch oven with a couple of tablespoons of butter. While they cooked, I chopped up a green pepper. That went into the pan as well with a pound of ground beef and another pound of ground pork. When the meat was cooked, I threw in three cans of crushed tomatoes and a tiny can of tomato paste. The tension in my shoulders began to relax as I added three cups of broth, Italian seasonings, and two bay leaves.

"Pasta sauce," I said as I looked down at what I was creating.

I brought it to a boil and then reduced the heat to simmer. The last step before I walked away for a couple of hours was to add some crushed garlic. I'd nearly forgotten.

It was just after seven when the sauce was done and my doorbell rang. I'd just finished draining the pasta and was dumping it back into the pot from the colander.

A quick glance out the front window told me it was Thorn. His truck was parked in my driveway, so I knew he'd had time to go home and change.

When I opened the front door, he pulled me into his arms and kissed me. "I've missed that," he said after a moment.

"I made pasta," I responded. "The sauce is almost from scratch."

"It smells delicious. I'm starving."

"Well, let's eat then."

We went into the kitchen, and Thorn poured us drinks and grabbed forks from the dishwasher. While he did that, I plated pasta and sauce for the two of us.

Dinner was quiet. The food was good, even if I did say so myself, and we were enjoying each other's company. Looking back, it was probably that we didn't want to break the spell. There were unpleasant things to discuss, but it was nice to have a few moments of happiness.

It didn't last forever, but it couldn't. While we were doing the dishes, Thorn brought it all up. I was washing, and he was drying.

"So, he kissed you, and you didn't kiss him back?" he asked as I handed him a clean plate to dry.

"I did. I didn't shove him away or hit him or anything. The whole thing was strange. I was so worried that you'd arrest him for something, and I'd never see him again. I mean, I was terrified and being near him felt urgent. It doesn't make sense looking back. It was as if he was someone I knew much better. But when I woke up the morning that I called you, it was gone. I didn't think he was using any kind of magic on me, but maybe I'm naive. Maybe it's not magic in the sense of what I can do, but that doesn't mean he doesn't have some sort of powers."

"But you're not interested in finding out what the connection between you is?" Thorn asked.

"I mean… no. I guess I'm not. I'd like to find out why he had that effect on me, but I can do research about vampires for that," I said.

"Because you went back over there again. He's your alibi for the murder," Thorn said.

"I was distraught about you saying you had planned on dumping me, and I still felt connected to him at the time. I thought I'd at least want to be his friend, you know? It felt like the empathic connection was real."

"I'm sorry," Thorn said. "I pushed you away, and I pushed you into this. I should have been more open with you from the beginning. I should have told you I loved you sooner. I guess I didn't want to scare you away."

"That wouldn't have scared me away," I said.

"It doesn't help that I've been working so many nights lately. If I had tried harder to fill the deputy position instead of being so precious about it, I would have been there for you that night."

"But now you will. You're hiring this new woman. The one that reminds you of me." I tried to keep the jealousy and insecurity out of my voice, but the look on Thorn's face told me instantly that I'd failed.

"You know when you say it that way, it sounds like I meant something I didn't," Thorn said. "I'm sorry I made you feel that way."

"But she could replace me, right?" Why not just lay it out there? "You said she reminds you of me, and she hasn't made the mistakes I've made. How could I not feel a little insecure?"

"I've definitely gone and put my foot in my mouth again, Kinsley. And no one could replace you. Not ever. I just meant that she's strong and independent. I'll be able to count on her to work at night so I can be with you. I mean, it's not like I'll be working with her other than the shift hand-off. What's going on, honey? I've got other female deputies. It's never made you feel bad."

"I think it just hit me the wrong way," I said. "The timing of it all, and the info came to me as a text. So, I let my imagination run wild. It wasn't anything you did."

Before Thorn could say anything else about our relationship, there was a knock at the door. Meri came skittering in from the dining room.

"Were you expecting anyone?" Thorn asked.

"I wasn't. Viv and Reggie were going to call, but I doubt either of them had plans to drop by. Pretty sure my family would call or text first. Except maybe Lilith. You never know with her."

"It's a vampire," Meri said.

"He's here," Thorn said, and I couldn't tell if it was an accusation or a question.

"Probably. Unless it's your contact looking for you," I said. "But that wouldn't make sense. Yeah, it's probably him. I haven't heard from him since he carted off my swag bags and decorations."

The knock came again.

"I'll answer it," Thorn said.

"What are you going to say?" I asked.

"I guess that depends on what he wants."

Thorn opened the door, and the look on Azriel's face was surprise. He quickly regained his stone-faced demeanor even as his eyes flicked to me and then back to Thorn. I wasn't sure why he was confused, though. Thorn's truck was in the driveway. Unless Azriel had just never paid any attention to Thorn.

"How can I help you?" Thorn asked in his sheriff voice.

"I'm here to talk to Kinsley," he said. "Can she come out and play?" Something in Azriel's voice was childish and taunting. Was he really trying to pick a fight with Thorn? On my front porch?

"If you're not here for a reason, then I'm going to politely ask you to leave," Thorn said. "Once."

"Kinsley, could you come out here please?" Azriel said. "Surely you're not going to let this man speak for you."

It was then that I felt it. The link between us started to thrum like a heartbeat. I took a step back as if that was going to help. "Meri..."

"What is it?" Thorn asked. "What is he doing?"

I saw Azriel cock his head to the side. "Oh, so he knows. He knows our secrets."

"I know your secrets too, Azriel. I know that the anonymous call the night we raided your club actually came from inside of your club. Got a tip about that, and you and I are going to

184

have to have a sit-down soon to discuss the matter."

"What?" I asked.

"Yeah, Kinsley. The call we got about suspicious activity came from inside the club. The whole thing was a setup. What I haven't figured out yet was why," Thorn said.

"It was the same night my windows were smashed," I said to Thorn. "Did you have something to do with that?" I asked Azriel. "Did one of your men call the police to lure them all out to the clubhouse? Were you helping Astra?"

"I did no such thing," Azriel said. "I wouldn't do that to you. I'll get to the bottom of this."

"No," Thorn said. "I'll get to the bottom of this. You don't need another reason to come sniffing around here."

"I don't think that's up to you," Azriel said. "It's up to Kinsley, and I don't think she likes you telling her who she can and cannot see."

My anger had stiffened the empathic link and Meri must have been helping too, but I felt its tentacles reaching out for me again. It had begun to feel less like a mutual link and more like something invading me.

"I know what you are," I said to Azriel. "You're not just a vampire. You're a psychic vampire." I reached down unconsciously and grabbed the bag hanging from my belt loop. "You fooled me for a while, but you won't fool me again. All I want from you is my stuff back."

"Now, Kinsley, don't be that way," Azriel said.

"She's spoken her piece," Thorn interrupted. "All you need to do is tell the lady how you intend to return her property, and then you can be on your way."

"I don't have any of her property." Azriel was growing angry, and he was barely keeping it under wraps. "I have the property she gave me. I won't be returning that. It was a gift, after all."

"That's not what happened," I said.

"You might not want to play it that way," Thorn said. "Please don't forget who you are dealing with."

"Thorn, I think you're right. I don't know that Amelda would like the way he's acting," I said.

"I'm not sure that Brighton would be too happy either," Thorn said. "But really, he should be even more afraid of you."

It was obvious that either Azriel had forgotten who he was dealing with or he believed his hold over me was much stronger that it actually was. The realization crept across his face until his eyes lit up for a split second with fear.

"This is your decision?" Azriel asked me.

"So much for you not wanting me to make a decisions," I said. "Everything you said to me was BS, wasn't it? Never mind. Don't bother answering that. Yes, this is my decision. I'll expect delivery of my bags and decorations tomorrow. You can have your men bring them to my storeroom. I've no need to see you."

He looked like he was about to say something else, but Thorn cut him off. "There's nothing more to discuss here. Send your men with her property tomorrow, and I will contact you about our meeting."

Azriel stormed off after that. I was thinking about the connection between the anonymous call and my shop being broken into when Thorn closed the door.

I didn't get to say anything before he pulled me into his arms and kissed me. "I think we're going to be okay," he finally said.

While that was a huge relief to me, the break-in and Astra's death still weight heavily on my mind.

Chapter Eight

The next morning shortly after we opened, Fortuna came into the shop. I had a huge envelope of cash that Meri had helped me find in the books in the attic. I showed Fortuna the receipts and totals, and when she agreed to the price, I slid the manila envelope across the counter to her.

"I found the laptop..."

"No, don't," she said. "There's no reason to discuss it."

"I did find something on it that I have to ask you about," I said. "If that's okay."

"Go ahead. Though I don't know how much help I can be."

I opened it back up again. "This folder is called photoes," I said and clicked on it. "It's full of pictures of people. Do you have any idea what it was about?"

"That is unusual," she admitted. "But I have no idea. I don't know what Astra was into."

"Well, thank you anyway," I said.

"No, thank you. You've really helped me out by buying these things," she said and fished a ring of keys from her purse. "Here are the keys to the shop. The lease is paid until the end of the month. I assume you can retrieve the items by then? At the end of the month, the landlord will come here to get the keys. I've already given her the instructions."

"Yes. We'll get everything tonight most likely. I'll hang onto the keys until the landlord gets them."

"Thank you again," Fortuna said before leaving.

When she was gone, Reggie came up to the counter. "Are we really getting all that stuff tonight. Do I get overtime for that?"

I laughed. "Of course you do. If you want to help, that is."

"Wouldn't miss it for the world," Reggie said.

It was a fairly slow day, and several times I considered closing the shop so we could get a head start on moving all of Astra's goods over to my store. But, every time I'd be ready to do it, a ghost tour would end and a few people would trickle in. Azriel's men showed up early in the afternoon and carried the boxes containing my swag bags and decorations to the storage room. Azriel didn't make an appearance and neither did the ghost, so the whole thing went smoothly enough.

By the time the store was ready to close, I wasn't much in the mood for moving a bunch of stuff. "I just want you to know that I'm going to use magic to pack up her store," I said to Reggie. "I can't use magic to move it over here, but I can use a spell to make the boxes feel lighter. Thorn's going to come with his truck."

"Let's do it," Reggie said.

"You're going to be okay watching me use magic?" I asked. "I'd think it would be a bit shocking at first."

"I'm looking forward to it, actually," Reggie said. "I'm curious to see if it's anything like the movies."

"Well, I hope I don't let you down," I said.

We walked across the square and I used the key to get into what had been Astra's shop. Reggie watched with fascination as I used a current of magic to float the boxes from the back to the front door. From there, we grabbed them and walked them out to Thorn's waiting truck.

"I can't believe how light this is," Reggie said. "It's like there's nothing in this box, but I can see it with my own eyes."

"Much better than schlepping boxes the hard way," I said.

Meri cleared his throat. If a cat can clear their throat. It was more like he mimicked the sound of a person clearing their throat. "Personal gain."

"Oh, man," I said. "I mean, is it really personal gain? I'm just making it easier for us. I'm not profiting."

"You're probably right," Meri said. "Guess we'll find out."

"You are such a butt," I said.

"Yeah, don't be such a square, Meri," Reggie said. "It's the same as using magic to do cleaning. Oh my gawd! I bet cleaning is so easy for you."

"I try not to use magic unless I have to," I said. "Well, except right now. I guess that rule is going right down the drain."

"I knew it would never last," Meri snarked.

"Quiet, cat," I said but I laughed at him nonetheless.

"Let's get this done," Thorn said. "You and the cat can fight it out later."

"I'd totally win," Meri said.

"I'm sure you would."

It took a few hours to take all of the truckloads of boxes over to my store. When the boxes from the storeroom were mostly moved, Thorn and Reggie finished loading them while I used magic to pack up the stock that was out on the shelves. Around nine that night, we were just about done moving things.

I went into what had been Astra's office and found that Fortuna hadn't cleaned it out. I hadn't paid for anything in the office, and I had no use for Astra's old paperwork, so I just left everything. The landlord would probably take the cleaning fee out of whatever deposit Astra had paid. Either way, it wasn't any of my business.

Something did catch my eye as I was shuffling around the folders on her desk. One of them had a word written across it in black Sharpie. "Charitie."

"That's weird," I said. "Something else she misspelled."

Unable to avoid my curiosity, I opened the folder. They were tax statements from a charity. More specifically, a cat rescue charity. Under the tax statements were photocopies of canceled checks from the bank. Astra had made the checks out to "Familiar Paws Kat Rescue" but the name of the charity was actually Familiar Paws Cat Rescue. She'd misspelled the word cat on every check.

"Huh," I said and closed the folder. I didn't know what it meant, so I made the executive decision to take the folder with me.

Reggie yawned and stretched after we carried the last of the boxes into my store. "I'd ask about getting something to eat, but I think I'm too tired. I'm just going to go home and shove some Fritos into my mouth with both hands before falling into bed."

"Sounds like a plan," I said.

When she was gone, Thorn asked me, " What about you? Do you just want to go home and eat some chips, or would you like to have a late dinner at Bella Vita with me?"

194

"Maybe just some toasted ravioli and a glass of wine," I said.

"That sounds excellent," Thorn replied.

"I guess I'll just walk home then," Meri said sarcastically.

"You can come with us and stay in the car," I offered.

"No thanks," Meri groused.

"Hey, we'll take you home first," Thorn said. "You don't have to walk."

Meri just stared at him for a moment as if Thorn had three heads. "Fine," he finally said. "If it's not, you know, too much trouble."

We took Meri home and then headed to the restaurant. They were open until midnight, so even though it felt really late to me, they were still going to be serving for a couple more hours.

"It's a good thing I don't have to get up early for work," I said as Thorn pulled the truck into the nearly deserted Bella Vita parking lot.

"We don't have to do this if it's too late," he said. "I do have to be up early for work, but I figured another hour wouldn't hurt. Tomorrow's not a run day for me."

"I should do that too," I said in response. "Get up early and run every other day."

"I could come over the mornings I do it and we could run together," Thorn said.

"Whoa." I chuckled as I unbuckled my seatbelt. "It's still in the thinking-about-it stage right now. Let's not get ahead of ourselves."

That made Thorn laugh. He came around and opened my door for me followed by helping me down out of the truck.

We went inside and took a seat at the bar. There were only a handful of people inside the restaurant, but it still didn't feel right to take up a table when we were just getting drinks and an appetizer.

"I saw that your gift bags and decorations were back in the storeroom," Thorn said after we had our drinks and the bartender had put our order into the kitchen. "Did he give you any problems?"

"He didn't show up," I said. "Two of his men brought the stuff back and put it in my storeroom. They didn't even look at me sideways."

"That's good."

"So, how did you find out the suspicious activity call came from the clubhouse?" I asked.

"My guy inside tipped me off. He told me I should look into the source of the call, so I did."

"I think it's weird that happened and then my windows got smashed. Do you think Astra could have been working with someone in the MC?"

"And you think one of them killed her because she knew too much about their part in the theft of your gift bags?" Thorn asked.

"It sounds stupid when you say it like that," I admitted.

"I'm not saying it's stupid," Thorn said. "I just don't think that's why she was killed. And I don't think Jemma did it either. I'm not sure what happened to Reggie, but the state police didn't find anything in that glass. She might want to schedule a check-up with her doctor."

"They didn't find anything because it's a magic drug," I said. "I know it is. I just need to figure out what it is."

"Well, either way, I think those are dead ends when it comes to Astra's murder. I think she just paid someone in the MC to make that call so we'd all be at the clubhouse when she smashed your windows, but I don't believe she was killed over it."

Chapter Nine

I didn't feel like sleeping after Thorn dropped me off. My mind wouldn't let the whole thing with Jemma go, but the potion I'd made to help identify the flowers would take time to work.

I sat down on my sofa and picked up the laptop. Maybe there was more in there I missed, or perhaps if I studied the "photoes" harder, I could figure something out.

When I moved it, I revealed Astra's notebook. I'd either grabbed it by accident or completely forgotten I had it.

Frustrated at the lack of solid suspects in the case, I began to leaf through the pages again. Maybe Astra had left a trail to her killer. I could only hope.

I thought about doing a seance to contact Astra, but I knew it was unlikely she'd remember her killer. Plus, I didn't want her around. And the Midnight Magic Festival was coming up fast. I wanted the whole murder business out of the way before the festival.

The drawings were quite good. I hadn't appreciated them before, but upon further inspection, even I had to admit that Astra was an excellent artist.

One of the drawings clearly depicted Jemma. The detail and shading work were astounding. So good in fact that there was no dispute it was her. Nor could there be any question that the flower sticking out of the drink in her hand was one of the purple ones in the garden. The illustration was in black and white, but she'd captured the shape of the petals perfectly.

At some point, she must have offered Astra a glass of the lemonade she'd tried to use on Reggie and me. But why? Obviously, the event had left an impression on Astra because she'd drawn such a detailed picture of the event.

But what did it all mean?

The wine, heavy food, and long day started to catch up with me. I didn't even feel like walking upstairs to my bed, so instead I curled up on the sofa and pulled the afghan hanging over the back down over me.

When I woke up the next morning, I'd overslept by an hour.

My phone had gone dead because I hadn't put in on the charger when I went to sleep like I normally did. The only reason I didn't sleep longer was because Meri's hunger finally roused him.

I got him some breakfast, threw on a clean pair of jeans and a t-shirt, and went into the kitchen to see what I could make into a quick breakfast.

In the end, I decided it would be faster just to go to the Brew Station and get coffee and a sandwich. Fortunately, I was late enough that the morning rush was mostly over.

Viv got my latte and croissant sandwich in record time and even threw in a side of extra bacon free for Meri. "You look like you've already had a rough morning," she said with a smile.

"Do I look that bad?" I lamented.

"No, but you might want to redo your ponytail. It looks like you slept in it."

"Oh, crud. I didn't even look at my hair this morning. Thanks, Viv."

"What are friends for?"

I made a mad dash across the square and managed to get inside before Reggie showed up for work. I fixed my hair in the shop's bathroom and ignored the ghostly specter of a woman in a white dress with black hair standing behind me the entire time.

"Not today," I said. "Sorry."

When my hair no longer looked like ferrets had been wrestling in it, I went into my office to wolf down my sandwich and get some of my latte into me.

In between bites, I sent a text out to my Mom. It was a long text explaining the potion I made to identify the plant I found in Jemma's garden. When I checked the potion that morning, it had turned black. I had no idea what that meant, but I hoped she would.

I kept staring at the phone waiting for her to text or call back, but she must have either let her phone go dead or been busy, because I didn't get a response before it was time to open.

What I did have time to do was call Thorn and tell him what I found in the notebook. "I really think she had something to do with it, or at the very least, there was something more going on there than just Astra stealing her garden gnome," I said.

"Yeah, but what proof do you have, Kinsley? I need more than magical evidence and theories to make an arrest. I'm sorry. I will look into it further," Thorn said.

"Well, at least she's locked up," I said.

"She's not," Thorn said.

"What?"

"She was released. There's some sort of bug going around and the hospitals are overcrowded right now. The psychiatrist decided that she was fine and released her."

"So, I have to watch my back," I said.

"From what I understand, she was released into the care of a relative. Jemma's not coming back to Coventry right now. I've got some time to figure this out before you're in danger from her."

"Okay," I said. "I'm protected here anyway."

"Call me if you need me?" Thorn asked.

"I will."

"Hey, Kinsley."

"Yeah?"

"I love you."

"I love you too."

It was time to open the shop, but Reggie still hadn't shown up yet. I was about to call her, but I started walking to the front of the store to put out the "open" sign.

When I did, I saw her coming out of the Brew Station. She was walking quickly in my direction, but it took me a second to notice she didn't have a coffee or a bag in her hands.

Reggie burst through the door. "We have a problem."

"What is it? Are you okay?"

"I'm fine, but Viv is gone," she said breathlessly.

"What do you mean, Viv is gone?"

"Hank, the guy who's working with her today, said she went out back to take the garbage out, and she never came back in. He said she's gone. He's tried calling her phone and her house. She's just gone."

"Maybe she had to run an errand," I suggested, but a feeling of cold dread had formed in the pit of my stomach. "She might not be answering her phone because she's driving."

"They had a line to the door, Kinsley. She wouldn't have just left without saying something to Hank. I think something happened to her."

"Okay. Stay here. I think I know where to go," I said.

"Stay here? What if they come for me too?" she asked.

"Meri will stay with you," I said.

"No, I won't," he groused.

"Yes, you will. I'll be fine. I'll call Thorn and have him meet me. You stay here and protect Reggie. That's an order."

"Fine."

On my way out to the car, I called Thorn and told him where to meet me. He started to protest, but I informed him that if he didn't go, I'd handle it myself.

"I'll be there in a few minutes," he relented.

"Thanks!" I said, but in truth, I knew I could handle it without him.

By the time I reached Jemma's house and climbed the fence into her backyard, there was a new statue in the middle of the altar. It was a tiny Viv dressed in a blue and white pinafore dress wearing a little blue hat.

Only, it wasn't a statue. Much to my horror, I knew it was the actual Viv. She'd been shrunk down into a garden gnome.

They were all people that Jemma had turned into garden gnomes. If I hadn't seen the tiny version of Viv, it never would have snapped into place for me.

That was why Astra had been left on my porch posed weird with a drink in her hand. Jemma had been trying to turn her into a gnome too, but it didn't work. She hadn't been able to turn her because Astra was a witch, but Jemma's Fae magic killed her in the process.

I didn't recognize the plants or the poison she'd used because it was Fae magic and trickery.

What I did know was that I had to turn Viv back quickly, and then I had to figure out how to turn all the rest of the gnomes back into people. The longer they stayed that way, the harder it would be to reverse the spell.

I ran across the flowerbeds, hopping over the circular rows of gnomes, as carefully as I could so as not to kick them, so I could get to Viv. The purple plants actually reached out and used their thorns to try to hold onto my pant legs, but I shook them off. Some of them I wilted with a withering stare. At least the darkness and chaos inside of me could be used for some good.

When I grabbed Viv's statue, I used what little chaos magic I knew to reverse the Fae magic. My darkness could override the trickery used to turn her, and I could definitely overpower any nature magic with it.

Suddenly, Viv was back. She stood in front of me with eyes as wide as saucers.

"What just happened?"

"I'll tell you soon, I promise. Right now, we have to find the woman who did this to you. We can't let her get away."

"All of these people..." Viv said despondently. "How is this possible?"

She was going into emotional shock. "Viv, it's going to be okay. My family and I can change them all back, I promise. We have to catch Jemma, though. She'll do this to more people."

"You're a witch. Like for real! That's so cool!"

"It's pretty cool," I said and patted her shoulder. "Did you see where she went?"

"She's right there. Inside," Viv said and pointed to the back door.

I turned and could see Jemma picking up gnomes and shoving them into a duffle bag. She didn't want to leave her gnomes behind.

"Stay out here," I said to Viv. "I only know a little about Fae magic, and I don't want her to turn you into a tree or something. You've been through enough."

Viv nodded, and I ran for the back door. It was locked, but that wasn't enough to stop me. A little magic and the doorknob turned.

"Stop right now!" I yelled at Jemma. "It's over!"

She picked up a pitcher of bright green liquid from the buffet in front of her and tried to fling its contents at me. "You were supposed to go down for her murder. It was too perfect!"

I dodged most of the liquid, though a little landed on my arm. My arm hairs began to turn into tiny vines, but I was able to counteract the magic.

"Ugh, I really hate witches!" Jemma spat.

"Nothing you do is going to work on me," I said. "You might as well stop while you're ahead."

Jemma's face turned bright red. She started shrieking and tearing at her own hair. Realizing that she might hurt herself, I envisioned ghostly green vines coming out of the floor and wrapping around her.

Why did I use vines? It served two purposes. The first was that it held her in place so she couldn't rip out her hair or scratch her face. The other was that she found the soft glowing vines soothing and stopped her ear-splitting shrieking.

Just about the time I got her quieted down, Thorn showed up. "You should have stayed outside," he said sternly.

"I had to get her. She'd turned Viv into a garden gnome. Thorn, all of these gnomes are people, and I believe Astra figured that out somehow. Jemma tried to turn Astra into a gnome too, but she's a witch. She couldn't do it. That didn't stop her from giving Astra more and more of the poison until she died," I said. "Why she was on my porch, I'm still trying to wrap my head around."

"Because everybody in town heard you were fighting," Jemma said. She was suddenly icy cool and calm. It was unnerving. "It's as simple as me trying to frame you. Why do you witches always have to be searching for meaning in things? It's one of your more annoying traits."

"This isn't going to go well," Thorn said.

"What do you mean?"

"Well, although she's mostly admitted she poisoned Astra, there's no evidence of that," he said. "The state police lab didn't find anything, and they won't. I think they're practically ready to rule Astra's death a heart attack or something. The official story being that she was waiting on your porch and died of natural causes or something like that."

"You're kidding me," I said.

"I wish I was."

I took a deep breath and stifled a sigh. "Then let them," I said. "If the death isn't ruled a murder, then no one will look into it further."

"Should I leave?" Thorn asked.

"Yeah," I said. "I'm going to call my family. I'm going to need them to help set these people free, and I'm sure Amelda and Lilith will have some interesting ideas on how to deal with Jemma."

Epilogue

Midnight Magic Festival

Viv was so excited about the Midnight Magic Festival really being magic that I had to keep reminding her she couldn't tell anyone. I didn't get mad at her, though. She'd been through so much, and for her, finding out that magic was real was like waking up on Christmas morning every single day. After all, she hadn't opened a witch-themed coffee shop for no reason.

The day of the festival, Reggie and I set up tables outside of the shop. We lined them with the swag bags, and Reggie watched to make sure people only took one. I worked inside the store for a few hours.

Eventually, as afternoon began to turn into night, we closed the shop and joined the festivities. A band set up in the middle of the square, and several local restaurants had food tents. There was a large cash bar as well that served regular drinks to the regular folks and magic elixirs to the witches.

Thorn was working that evening because the sheriff's office had to provide security, but he kept stealing away to dance with me and give me kisses. We'd twirl around in circles to the music until we were both dizzy and gasping for breath, and then he'd go on patrol again.

My entire family was there, and they welcomed Reggie and Viv into the fold with open arms. They could never be witches, but they were now our sisters. Meri stuffed himself so full with bacon that he slinked off to sleep near one of the columns on the front steps of the courthouse.

I was dancing with Reggie to the beat of some zydeco song while we laughed and drank fizzy pink drinks when I saw Azriel. None of his MC had shown up at the festival. Word around town was that they'd gotten on their motorcycles and rolled out of town, so he was the last person I expected to see.

But he was there watching me. His gaze was so heavy that I could almost feel it like weight. "I'll be back," I said to Reggie.

"Will you be okay?" she asked when Azriel fell into her line of sight.

"I'll be fine. It's him you need to worry about," I said.

"I can only imagine," she said. "Don't get yourself arrested without me."

I chuckled and then walked in Azriel's direction. When he saw me coming toward him, he disappeared around the corner. I wasn't sure if he'd fled when he saw me coming or just wanted more privacy.

It turned out he was still there. "What do you want?" he asked me harshly.

"What do you mean, what do I want? You're the one hanging out in the shadows watching me," I said.

"If I was truly in the shadows, you never would have seen me," he said.

"Whatever, Azriel. Why are you watching me?" I asked.

"I don't know," he said, and he sounded so dejected that it almost seemed real. "I should go."

"Before you do, could you at least have the decency to tell me why you helped Astra destroy my shop and steal my stuff?" I said.

"I never said that I did."

"Well, just then, you didn't deny it. So, I'm pretty sure that's as close as I'm ever going to get to a confession. I just hope you didn't hurt Tangerine to lure me to your place. You will wish for death if I ever find out you hurt that dog," I hissed.

"Now, there's the Kinsley I admire," he said with a wistful smile. "I love your dark side, beautiful girl. No, I would never hurt Geri. That was real. It didn't set things in motion. It just changed the course of things a little."

"But why, Azriel? Why?"

"Because she had money and I wanted you within my grasp again. It was a mutually beneficial business relationship."

As I walked away from him, his words *I love your dark side, beautiful girl*, cut me like a knife. As I lay there in bed that night, I couldn't sleep. Those words just kept ringing in my head.

I eventually got up and went downstairs. After making a cup of hot chocolate, I settled in on the sofa to wait for the sun to come up.

Astra's notebook still sat on my coffee table. I opened it up and began studying the drawings as I sipped my cocoa. They made a great deal more sense once I knew what had happened.

My Aunties had extracted the truth from Jemma before they turned her into a little pink and purple fairy and put her in a jar, a curiosity to sit on Lilith's mantle until she passed on and the jar passed down to me.

Astra had come to Coventry to find Jemma. That gnome she'd stolen, it was her fiancé. Her human fiancé. He'd decided to stay in Coventry.

A great many of the people we freed did, but some left. They went home awakened from what they believed was some sort of fugue state. The official working hypothesis according to the nightly news is that some sort of virus caused thousands of people to go into an amnesiac state. As soon as they recovered, they returned to their friends and families with no memory of what happened. Scientists are still working to find the actual virus. They can't, and the new theory is that it's a prion disease, like mad cow, instead. It will be forgotten within two news cycles. Life will go on.

There was good in everyone. That was a lesson Astra taught me. She tried to ruin my business, but she loved her fiancé fiercely. She also donated money to homeless familiars. Kats.

Apparently, she was a dark witch from birth, but she tried to be good, and when she did, it gave her a form of dyslexia. Imagine that.

Being so bad that your brain literally short-circuits when you do something good.

But she did try. There was love in her heart. But I couldn't think about that. I had to push those thoughts aside.

Because if there was good in her... if there was love in her heart... then she couldn't be the only one.

I love your dark side, beautiful girl.

Thank you for reading!

Made in United States
Orlando, FL
01 February 2024

43153274R00131